Terry Wise's Introduction to Battle Gaming

Including his unpublished wargaming rules

Edited by John Curry

This first part of his book was first published in 1969 as *Introduction to Battle Gaming* by Allied Publications Ltd. The rules in part two are Terry Wise's own rules that until now have been unpublished.

This edition printed 2010

Copyright © 2010 John Curry and Shirley Wise

All rights reserved. No part of this book may be reproduced or transmitted in any form by any means, electronic, mechanical, photocopying, recording, or otherwise without the prior written permission of authors.

Books edited by John Curry as part of the History of Wargaming Project
Army Wargames: Staff College Exercises 1870-1980.
Charlie Wesencraft's Practical Wargaming
Charlie Wesencraft's With Pike and Musket
Donald Featherstone's Lost Tales
Donald Featherstone's War Games
Donald Featherstone's Skirmish Wargaming
Donald Featherstone's Naval Wargames
Donald Featherstone's Advanced Wargames
Donald Featherstone's Wargaming Campaigns
Donald Featherstone's Solo Wargaming
Donald Featherstone's Wargaming Airborne Operations
Donald Featherstone's Lost Tales
The Fred Jane Naval Wargame (1906) including the Royal Navy War Game (1921)
Paddy Griffith's Napoleonic Wargaming for Fun
Sprawling Wargames: Multi-player wargaming by Paddy Griffith
Verdy's 'Free Kriegspiel' including the Victorian Army's 1896 War Game
Tony Bath's Ancient Wargaming
Phil Dunn's Sea Battles
Peter Perla's The Art of Wargaming
And many others

See The History of Wargaming Project at www.wargaming.co for a continually expanding range of wargaming publications.

ISBN 978-0-557-12097-0

Contents

Reflections on a lifetime of wargaming	5
Terence (Terry) Wise 1936-2010 An appreciation by Stuart Asquith	9
Part I Introduction to Battle Gaming	**13**
CHAPTER 1 THE ORIGINS OF BATTLE GAMING	15
CHAPTER 2 CHOOSING YOUR ERA	21
CHAPTER 3 BASIC BATTLEFIELD LAYOUT	39
CHAPTER 4 ADDING REALISM TO YOUR LAYOUT	54
CHAPTER 5 ORGANISING YOUR ARMY	62
CHAPTER 6 THE RULES FOR ANCIENT WARFARE	76
CHAPTER 7 THE RULES FOR THE HORSE AND MUSKET ERA	92
CHAPTER 8 THE RULES FOR MODERN WARFARE (2ND WORLD WAR)	101
CHAPTER 9 VARIATIONS OF THE GAME	113
CHAPTER 10 SOME IDEAS FOR ADVANCED PLAYERS	118
Part II Wargaming Rules of Terry Wise	**127**
18TH CENTURY RULES	129
NAPOLEONIC WARGAMING RULES 1792-1815	134
COLONIAL RULES 1874 – 1914	147

Reflections on a lifetime of wargaming

Born in London in 1935, the first thing I remember is an ARP warden riding past our house on a bicycle, shouting "War Declared." The war seems to have coloured my life. After the London Blitz, doodlebugs and other wartime experiences, at 13 I joined the Sea Cadets as my family had naval traditions. After five years of being with the Sea Cadets, I joined the Army and served in Centurion Tanks with the 17th /21st Lancers. After being in the navy and then the army, I did the obvious, which was to run away to sea and went on three whaling expeditions to the Antarctic.

By the time I returned from these Antarctic adventures everyone I knew from my immediate friends was married and respectable, so I settled down in the book trade, rising to the giddy heights of Sales Manager. After nine years, I decided I didn't want to do this as a life long career after all, and became an author.

I wished to write fiction, some say I never wrote anything else, but I instead finished up writing military history for the next 15 years. Between 1967 and 1982, I wrote some 40 books and over 400 articles on military history and related subjects. The problem with being an author was making enough money to survive, so I then returned to bookselling (but specializing in military history) in order to feed a family which had occurred en route. I set up Athena Books in 1981, Selling military history books was far more interesting that the regular book trade.

I returned home one day in the early 1960's to discover two nephews playing with little plastic Airfix soldiers. At this time I was keen on photography, so I bought some figures, painted them, posed them, moved them about, photographed them, and thus I believed I had invented wargaming. Imagine my chagrin when, during a visit to the local library, I discovered the great works of *Little Wars* and *Featherstone's War Games*[1].

My interest in wargaming spread from the American Civil War to World War 2, then back to Ancients. The latter was inspired by my youth, as I had read all the Greek & Roman classics during my early teens. Since those early days, I have spent my time filling in the gaps in my wargaming interests, so I now have figures from 1800 BC to AD 1945. However, I do restrict myself by avoiding anything Eastern (except for Persians, Saracens, Boxer Rising . . .)

Some say I have accrued a somewhat large collection of figures. However, I have no idea of exactly how many; I once 'lost' my Crimean collection for over a year! Probably about 25,000, but that is only a guess. I prefer to play with the figures not count them.

---

[1] Reprinted by the History of Wargaming Project

Given the cooperation of the manufacturers, I would wargame exclusively in 20mm: it is the perfect scale for me, with figures large enough to retain the toy soldier appeal, but small enough for large battles. I still use 20mm for 1700-1945, with 25mm for earlier periods. Many 25mm have crept into the post-1700 collection over the years, as one has to conform to opponents' collections.

My favourite period is wargaming 1800BC to AD1945; but probably my absolute favorite period has been the Horse and Musket period 1700-1815. Since retirement, I have concentrated more on the Napoleonic period and have reduced my collection in this area to only circa 5,000 20mm Napoleonic's[2].

Over a lifetime of wargaming, I have always preferred to write my own rules. Most wargamers I know read commercial rules for ideas: they rarely use the rules as published. I fear influence from such rules, and never read or use commercial rules if I can avoid it, lest they influence my thinking. I prefer to read all I can on a period, then try to recreate it on the tabletop. The basic aims are to reward those who use correct tactics, penalize those who use incorrect or poor tactics. Also, decisions must be placed in the hands of the players, NOT made by the rules. I believe in warGAMES: the better player should win on his merit. Inexperienced Players usually learn quickly - by their mistakes. A good example is artillery firing: player' have to assess range - their skill decides whether they hit the target, not the throw of a mere dice.

The wargames books that have influenced me the most were Peter Young's *Charge!* and H.G. Wells' *Little Wars*; they have inspired my emphasis on the game element and simple rules. However, for the past 40 years or so I have been unable to use their rules for my own games as I find them too reliant on pure chance: I prefer solo whist to vingt-et-un.

I am not of the mainstream hobby, but would say the most influential commercial rules were those of the Wargames Research Group (WRG). They have had the most effect on wargaming throughout the world. They should be praised for this, but it is a pity alternative types of gaming were not offered during the 1970's.

Between 1960 and 1990, the hobby continued to change When I started wargaming there was Airfix (or Hinton Hunt or the excellent figures of Scruby for the rich.) Accessories had to be hunted down in model railway shops. It was fun creating games. Today the wargamer can buy anything they desire, and availability removes some of the enjoyment. The change is summed up by a display I saw at a recent convention: a medieval siege using commercially produced terrain squares, castle and buildings, with a few well painted figures - painted commercially. All the wargamers had provided was money. The display looked good, but dead; it could have belonged to anyone - individuality

---

[2] It is, of course, difficult to imagine how one would cope with less than 5,000 figures for a single period. Editor.

has been erased. In the future we shall be offered even more irresistible selections of figures and accessories, in a multiplicity of scales (which do not match between manufacturers), so that we shall become even more dissatisfied with the silver mountains of unpainted figures which we have already collected at vast expense. At some point we shall have to say "NO!" I will keep what I have and enjoy it: I will not succumb to the evils of temptation." Maximum satisfaction probably lies in concentrating on one major war, sticking to one scale and manufacturer, and isolating oneself from commercial influences. However, this is not nearly so much fun as visiting a convention and emerging clutching plastic bags full of bits of metal, which you didn't really want anyway.

The best part of wargaming, for me, are campaigns as they offer playing with toy soldiers, but wrestling with 'real' problems in tactics and strategy. The part I enjoy least is painting figures - but look at the rewards!

Some of my best ever wargames were with my local group, between 1978-1990. The Doncaster Fanatics was formed because we shared a dislike of the small, short games being played at the local club. The Fanatics consists of myself and three friends, who wargame at my house every Friday night, with occasional all day games and displays at conventions. For us, this is the perfect type of wargaming. Originally we put on displays **in** order to carry The Word to the savages outside the pale, but wargaming is now pretty well set in its style, and we are becoming more isolationist. Our latest idea is to stop preaching to the converted, and seek non-wargamers who may be converted. We ran a campaign every winter, break up very large games with small skirmish ones, do a fair bit of converting and scratch building, and generally enjoy ourselves. Who could ask for more? For me, wargaming has been a life long hobby.

Terence (Terry) Wise 1936-2010 An appreciation by Stuart Asquith

I first met Terry Wise in the early 1970,s by which time he'd served on Centurion tanks in Germany with the 17th/21st Lancers and had also been on two whaling expeditions.

Terry's writing career began in 1967 and over the next fourteen years or so he was to write no less than forty books and in excess of four hundred articles for magazines. Among Terry's many books were his very popular and influential *Introduction to Battle Gaming* (MAP 1969) which many people cite as their starting point in the hobby, *American Civil Wargaming* in the Airfix 'Guides' series, his six part *Battles for Wargamers* series for Bellona (MAP 1972-1974) and more than twelve titles for Osprey Publishing including *Flags of the Napoleonic Wars* (three volumes), *Armies of the Crusades*, and *1066 Year of Destiny*. Terry was instrumental in commissioning my very first book *The Campaign of Naseby 1645* (1979) in his capacity as editor of the short lived Osprey Wargames Series.

Terry also made the masters for the Bellona range of plastic vac-formed items of wargames terrain. His well known monthly *Observation Post* column in *Military Modelling* magazine featuring hobby news, reviews and chat began in 1977; I was privileged to take over this feature from Terry in 1981, seeing it through until its cessation in 2001.

Terry also wrote extensively in *Airfix Magazine* with popular series on such subjects as converting Airfix buildings and *Operation Sea Lion* as a war game.

Terry was very fond of the 1/72 scale Airfix figures and had, until the advent of the Hinton Hunt and Les Higgins/Phoenix Model Developments ranges, quite literally, thousands of them in various periods. It was he who suggested adding a scratch built howdah to the baby elephant from the (now defunct) Britain's series of zoo animals and using the beast as a war elephant.

After moving from Gloucestershire to Doncaster, Terry began buying and selling second hand military books, but the stock soon outgrew the family home and he opened Athena Books as a retail premises in Doncaster in 1981. Also for a time his 'Wargamer's Den' selling war game figures, paints etc. flourished from the first floor of the family home and the 'Doncaster Fanatics' had frequent meetings at his house.

Terry and I had a number of games in his lean-to barn in Lydney, usually Napoleonic and always with hundreds of Airfix figures. I fondly recall one particular Napoleonic battle – Borodino was it? – that I won. Afterwards Terry admitted that it was the movement of my reserve cavalry so early in the game that threw his battle plan. I had to confess that said cavalry, positioned near my base line, were moved simply to make room for my elbows...

On another occasion, also in the 1970's, I and two other members of the Rayners Lane War Games Group headed north from London to put on a game at the first Eboracum show staged in York by our good friend Keith 'Genghis' Benson. En route we picked up Terry in Doncaster and continued on our journey. The game was an 18th century set-to using (what else?) Spencer Smith figures and *Charge!* rules. Well, we set the figures out, Terry and I facing the other two lads. Their opening artillery salvo destroyed both our guns – Terry and I just looked at one another as the other two fell about laughing.

Terry and I also conducted a long running postal campaign set in the era of the French Revolution.

In the 1970's and 1980's, Terry, Charlie Wesencraft and I used to get together once a year for a long weekend's wargaming at one another's homes. In 1980 Terry became a god parent of our son and always kept an eye on his progress.

In 1984 Terry's wife Shirley started Imperial Press which produced a number of wargame publications under the Athena Wargames Rules banner, including his *The English Civil Wars and the Thirty Years War* and my own *Marlburian Warfare 1702-1714* (1986) as well as Shirley and Terry's own well received *A Guide to Military Museums* which ran to several editions in successive years.

Terry sold Athena Books in 1991 and started Terence Wise Military Books, which specialised in the reprinting of 18th century military titles. The company was re-named and transferred to his daughter in 2000.

A move to Wales followed, where Terry and his wife enjoyed retirement before finally moving back to Doncaster to be closer to their family. Five months after being diagnosed with lung cancer, Terry died at home on 17th August 2010. Thus passed away one of the founding fathers and leading lights of the hobby, whose contribution to war gaming was considerable and whose enthusiasm never waned over all the years.

Terry was, to me, a valued friend of many years standing and the hobby will mourn his passing. It is pleasing to know that Terry's memory will be preserved with the publication of this present work which includes three sets of previously unpublished war game rules written by him.

Terry leaves his wife Shirley, their two grown up children, Rachel and Edward, and their respective families. May I on behalf of the many people who appreciated Terry the man, Terry the writer and Terry the wargamer pass on our sincere condolences in this time of their sad personal loss.

Those wishing to make a donation to commemorate Terry's life might like to consider making a donation direct to the Red Cross, Marie

Curie Cancer Care, Macmillan Nurses or Cancer Research UK in his name.

Stuart Asquith
August 2010

Part I Introduction to Battle Gaming

Chapter 1 The Origins of Battle Gaming

Colonel Custer rode forward and stood in his stirrups to peer down into the Little Big Horn valley. Below him lay the villages, the last of the Indians just riding off to join in the fight with Major Reno's command at the northern end of the valley. Here was the moment he had planned for over the past four days. Here lay the opportunity to recapture the President's favour! He turned back to his saddle-weary troopers.

"We've got them! We've caught them napping!" he cried triumphantly and his men cheered him hoarsely.

The battle flag was unfurled, cinches tightened. Eagerly Custer led the five troops of his beloved 7th Cavalry down Medicine Tail Coulee to destroy the now unguarded Indian villages and charge the unsuspecting hostiles from the rear. Not one man of his command was ever seen alive again. . .

Military looking chess set from Rajasthan, India

The battle of the Little Big Horn is surely familiar to everyone—you have probably read a book or seen a film about it at some time. Was Custer a fool to go charging blindly to the attack? Did he get what he deserved, or did his famous luck merely run out? Would *you* have acted differently had you been in his position? Historians can give us few definite facts about the battle but, given the knowledge Custer is believed to have had at that time, could you have done any better?[3]

Early toy soldiers: Egyptian troops of painted wood from the tomb of Masahite, Prince of Asiout, 11th Dynasty, 2100-2000 B.C.

Here is your chance to find out, for it is hoped that by the time you have read this book you will be fully capable of taking command of a regiment of cavalry and soundly thrashing 4,000 Sioux! Given the introduction to battle gaming—complete with a basic set of rules, such as this book contains—there need be no limit to the era into which you venture. You can be Caesar at the dreadful siege of Alesia, Alexander terribly outnumbered at Arbela, or Patton fighting stubbornly at the Battle of the Bulge against the German Army's last great Blitzkrieg. You can 'stonewall' with Jackson at First Bull Run, give Wellington's boot to Napoleon or change world history and reverse the result of Stalingrad. The only limit is your ambition.

---

[3] Modern battlefield archeology has now dissected the battlefield down to working out what was fired from which position (from the shell cases) to where they were aiming at (from the unique marks on the bullets) allowing a very detailed reconstruction of the battle to be made.

Metal figures made by the German Allgeyer about 1877.

Polystyrene figures made by Airfix and adapted to represent an army in ancient times.

Battle games are really as old as history—boys are known to have had toy soldiers as far back as 4,000 years ago—and have been played in a small way ever since the first boy sat down with a few models to recreate his father's wars.

Then in 1824 a Prussian officer invented a military game called Kriegsspiel and battle gaming on a serious level had begun. The Prussian Army game was played with three large-scale maps, each of the players having one and the third held by an umpire. Three rooms were used and troops were represented by red and blue blocks.

A medieval siege in full swing using 20 mm Airfix figures.

Senior officers presented the players with objectives, the players drew up their plan of campaign and these were passed to the umpire. Each player then set his pieces on his map, the umpire placing the pieces of both players on his map. Now the game began with alternate moves, the umpire placing opposing pieces on the players' maps as they became visible according to the map contours. By this method the players could see only what a general on the spot would see.

Casualties from firing and any advantages gained were decided by the umpire and the game continued until one player had been manoeuvred into a position of defeat. Using this 'game' the Prussian General Staff planned the strategy that defeated the French in 1870 and almost enabled them to capture Paris in the opening moves of the First World War. This purely military game was the beginning of battle gaming.

In 1913 H. G. Wells revolutionised the game. At the time of the Boer War Jerome K. Jerome was dining at the Wells' home when he spotted some of the children's toys on an adjacent table. Jerome lined up the soldiers and opened fire with a toy gun. He was so successful that he promptly issued a challenge and a fierce battle raged over the forgotten coffee cups. Later Jerome left and forgot the incident, but not so Wells. He began to ponder on the possibilities of the game and over the years improved his game until in 1913 he published a book called *Little Wars* which is still the battle gamer's main inspiration.

The British General Staff began to use battle games to train officers during the First World War and the military side of the game developed into the elaborate 'mock-ups' used in the Second World War, complete with all possible data supplied by aerial photography and secret agents.

A scene from the American Civil War with Federal troops attacking across a river. Figures are Airfix 20 mm

His Majesty's Land Ship! One of the first tanks shown here with World War I American infantry, all made by Airfix.

An American amphibious landing during the 2nd World War, reconstructed with Airfix figures

After the war a small band of enthusiasts kept the skill of battle gaming alive. The societies formed by these people are listed in an appendix, together with magazines and books written by them that will enable the newcomer to the hobby to make use of their vast experience.

Though this book is aimed at the younger newcomer, in the hope that the hobby will spread, there is no age limit to battle gaming. H. G. Wells sums it up admirably: *"Little Wars* is the game of kings—for players in an inferior social position. It can be played by boys of every age from twelve to a hundred and fifty—and even later if the limbs remain sufficiently supple—by girls of the better sort, and by a few rare and gifted women."

Chapter 2 Choosing your Era

Let us return for the moment to Colonel Custer. History tells us that Custer set out for the Little Big Horn after a conference with General Terry on June 22nd. His orders were to engage the Sioux on June 26th when General Terry's column would also attack, from the opposite direction.

Custer conducted his approach march with great caution, arriving undetected near the Little Big Horn on the evening of the 24th— no mean feat considering he had nearly 700 mounted men and a supply train of mules and wagons to move over dry and dusty land. But on the morning of the 25th this large column was spotted by the Sioux.

Custer was a successful Indian fighter and had proved his fighting ability as a cavalry leader in the Civil War. He was well supplied with Indian and white scouts who knew the terrain intimately and his 7th Cavalry was one of the finest regiments in the entire U.S. Army. The Sioux had been estimated at between 700 and 800 braves, and there was the common knowledge that they had never yet stood up to a direct fight.

The 7th cavalry's movements on June 25th

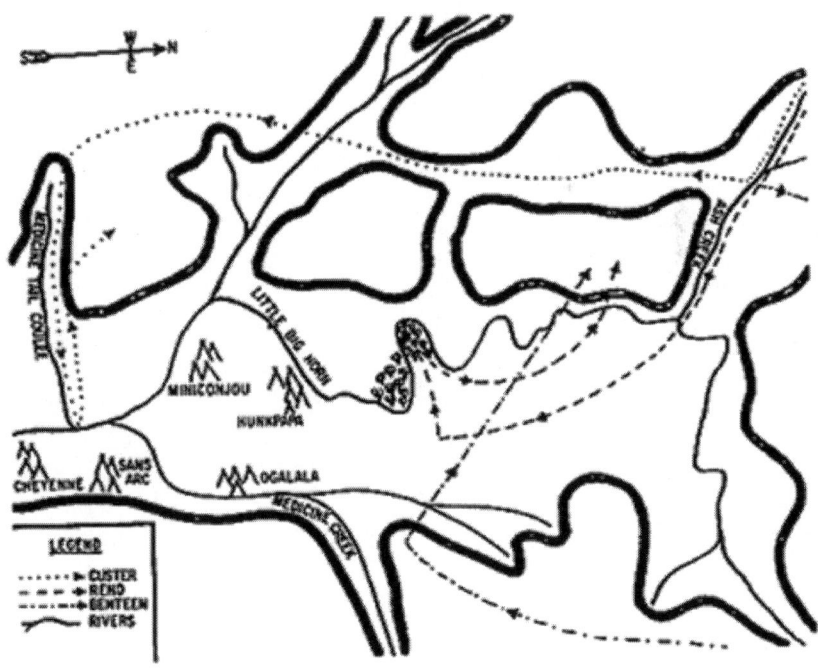

Custer's Last Stand- The traditional version reconstructed with Airfix figures

Not surprisingly Custer decided to charge into them before they could scatter and escape. He split his command into three squadrons, intending to let Major Reno draw the main assault to the north while he circled south to attack from the rear. Remember, this was a wild and lonely land, without modern means of communication and Custer expected to meet 800 Sioux at the most. Would you have waited 24 hours for the supporting column and risked letting the Sioux fade away into the hills, perhaps never to be brought to a confrontation again, or would you have charged in?

Custer has been branded a fool and a glory-seeker, and perhaps you thought he was mad to charge 4,000 Indians with only 224 men, but, as I have tried to illustrate, once you know the hard facts you begin to see things in a different light.

This is the real art of battle gaming, to re-fight a battle with the knowledge that the commander had *at that time.* Most battle gamers are military enthusiasts with a keen interest in history, for each battle requires considerable research into the real facts. Because of this the majority of players restrict their attention to one era of world history, although many purely fictitious games are also played that require no research.

For convenience military history can be roughly divided into three eras: the bow and arrow or Ancient era, the Horse and Musket era and modern times. In the following pages I have sketched out some battles to illustrate the possibilities of the different eras.

The main moves during the battle of Arbela, 331 B.C.

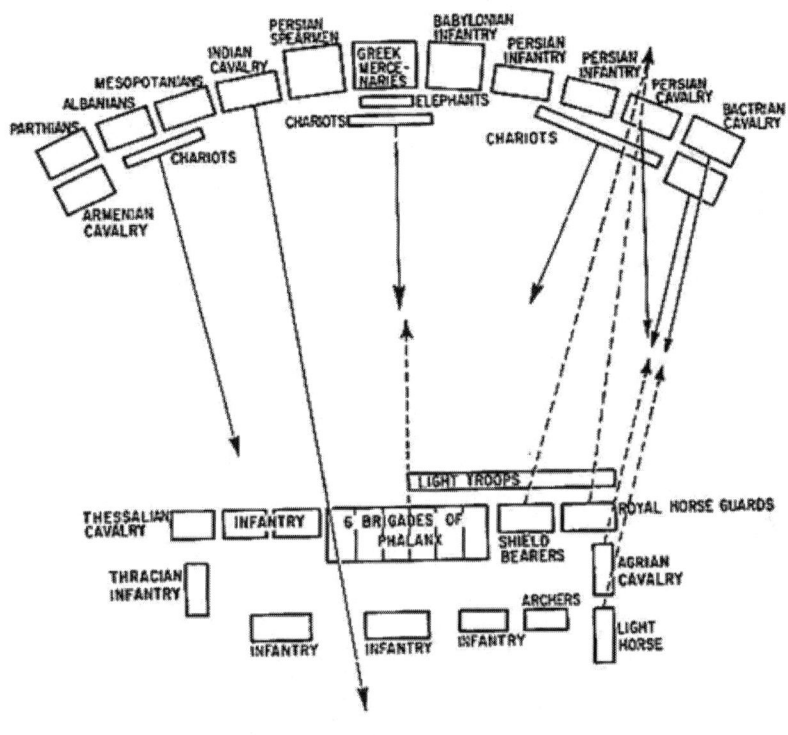

A reconstruction of the cavalry fights on Alexander's right flank.

The Napoleonic era is probably the most popular at present and with its sweeping manoeuvres and resplendent uniforms it is easy to understand why. The Second World War is a keen rival with its mass of different vehicles and weapons that provide the enthusiastic modeller with endless construction possibilities and the battle gamer with unending complications about weapons and their relative fire powers.

The Greek phalanx in the centre facing the Persian chariots and elephants which failed to break their formation.

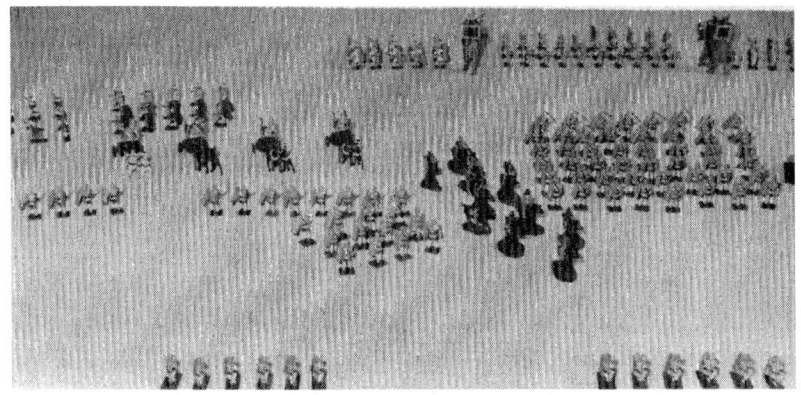

The Sikh-horsemen breaking through the Greek line, an opportunity that was lost by lack of discipline.

Another favourite is the American Civil War, the first major war where railways, telegraph, breech-loading guns and rifles, repeating rifles, announced ships, naval torpedoes and mines and a submarine were used. However, the era is a matter of personal taste. Once you have decided on the type of warfare you wish to specialise in you can begin to build up your model army—not before! As soon as you decide on the era I suggest you contact the appropriate society—they will be of great help, especially with research.

Arbela, 331 B.C.

In this battle Alexander the Great with 47,000 men faced the Persians and their allies with a total of 140,000 men to decide the fate of the mighty Persian empire. The Persian king, Darius, picked a flat open battlefield on which to spread his vast horde and waited for Alexander to attack him. He even went so far as to have some of the rough ground in front of his positions smoothed so that his chariots might charge faster.

Alexander's skirmishers captured some Persian scouts who revealed Darius' strength and positions and because of this intelligence Alexander rested his men for four days then advanced by night, intending to attack at dawn. However, the next morning he saw the levelled ground and, suspecting pitfalls for his cavalry, ordered a day of reconnaissance.

Alexander had no natural barriers to protect his flanks, which were overlapped by the Persian horde, so he formed a second line that could launch a counter-attack on either flank or face about in the event of complete encirclement.

At dawn the next morning he led his Royal Horse Guards to attack the Persian right wing, advancing obliquely so as to by-pass the edge of the levelled ground. Darius ordered his Scythian cavalry to stop this sideways movement but Alexander countered by bringing forward his Agrian cavalry. Both Darius and Alexander brought up their reserve cavalry and a fierce fight developed but eventually the Persians were beaten off.

Darius next ordered his chariots and elephants to soften up the Greek phalanx but most of them were stopped by skirmishers and the remainder were allowed to pass through the phalanx to the rear, where they were destroyed by the second line.

A second massed cavalry attack was launched against Alexander's right, the Bactrian cavalry trying to outflank the Greeks. However, they were themselves outflanked by the Greek light horse and another fierce struggle started, the Horse Guards being still uncommitted.

Suddenly a large body of Persian cavalry left their position on the left and without orders charged to assist the Bactrians. The Horse Guards charged into the gap, closely followed by the shield-bearing infantry, and began to press against the Persian left centre. At the same time the phalanx began its attack on the Persian centre.

At this critical moment the driver of Darius' chariot was killed by a javelin. The king ran to a nearby horse and rode from the field.

Meanwhile the Persian right had attacked the Greeks opposite to their position. Seeing this, one brigade of the phalanx fell back to protect the left's exposed right flank. In a flash a large body of Sikh horsemen charged through the resulting gap in the Greek line. They smashed right through the second line too but instead of turning to attack from the rear they galloped on to attack the lightly held Greek camp.

Alexander moved his Horse Guards across the battlefield to assist the left flank only to run into the Sikhs returning from his camp where they had been repulsed after a hard fight. A desperate struggle followed in which the Sikhs fought to the finish, wounding three of the generals round Alexander and killing some 60 of the elite Horse Guards.

By the time Alexander was able to reach his left flank the Persians there, deserted by their king, had fallen back, then broken and fled. Alexander ordered a pursuit which turned the Persian mass into a shattered rabble and, trapped by the River Lycus, the Persians lost more men in this rout than in the actual battle. No accurate figures are available of the casualties.

Agincourt, 1415

During the invasion of France Henry V with a small, starving army of 1,000 men-at-arms and 5,000 archers was intercepted by a French army of 24,000 men. Realising his hopeless position, Henry offered to make good all the damage he had inflicted if he might be allowed to leave France in peace. The French refused to negotiate.

The battle of Agincourt, 1415

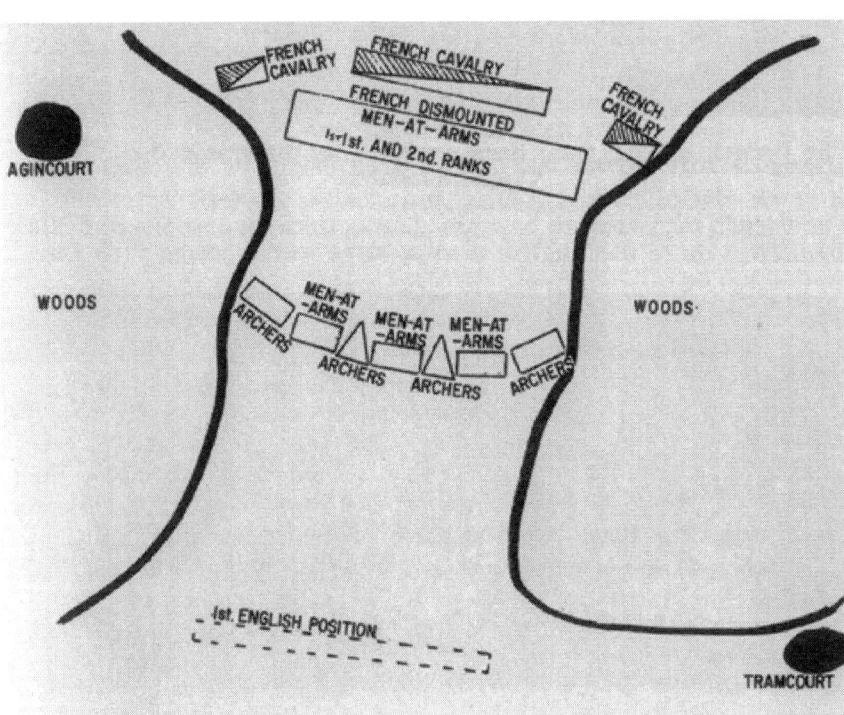

In this reconstruction, the English are just moving into bow range to force the French to attack

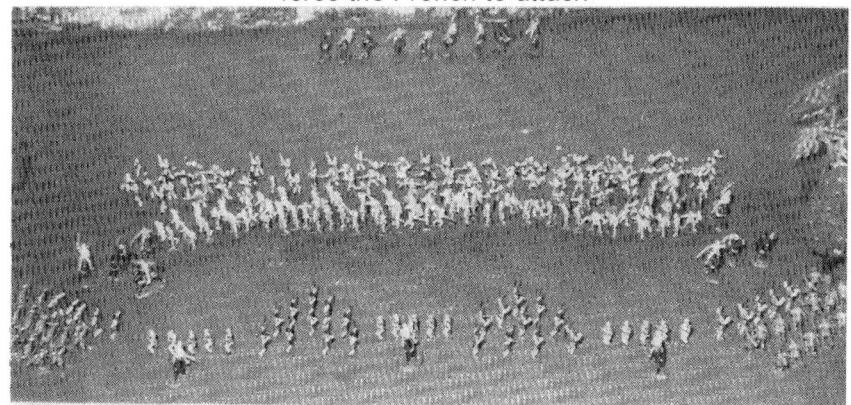

The French charge, their lines confused by the cramped and muddy space available.

The French men-at-arms have shied away from the archers, funnelling themselves on to the English men-at-arms and exposing their flanks.

The next day the French host formed up in three deep ranks with a body of about 600 cavalry on each flank and waited for the weak English army to attack. Henry knew he could not launch an attack so he moved his line forward until the French were within bow shot. As his archers planted their sharpened stakes and began to fire the cavalry on the French flanks advanced to the attack.

Those on the right made only a feeble attempt, many of them not even leaving their position. Those on the left charged home, but many horses, wounded by arrows, became uncontrollable and the knights retired from the fight. Those that reached the English line stumbled over the stakes and few ever rose again.

As the cavalry had charged, the French first and second lines had also advanced, the dismounted knights making poor progress through the muddy field in their heavy armour. The retreating cavalry ploughed through their own men, disorganising the ranks which were further confused by the narrowing front.

Cramped on each flank and with all formation lost the French men-at-arms blundered on, plagued by a heavy hail of arrows that forced them to keep their heads down, adding to the confusion. By sheer weight of numbers they forced the English line back a few feet but then, their exposed flanks harassed by archers, they ground to a halt.

The lightly armed archers swarmed over the helpless men-at-arms, many of whom were too tightly packed to even raise their weapons, and despatched them with axes and swords until the bodies lay three deep.

Several thousand prisoners had been taken and the battle was as good as won—the mounted French third rank having failed to attack—when it was reported that the English baggage train was under attack. In the resulting confusion the French prisoners, who outnumbered the English, began to rally again and Henry was forced to have them all killed.

A few men of noble birth in the third French line now attempted to charge home over the barrier of bodies, but they were all cut down and the rest, some 5,000 men, fled from the field.

French losses were estimated at about 6,000 men-at-arms killed and 1,000 taken prisoner. The common soldiers were never counted. English losses are not known but are not generally believed to have exceeded a few hundred.

Murfreesboro, 1862

During General Grant's campaign against the Confederate stronghold of Vicksburg, General Rosecrans with 44,000 men was sent to Murfreesboro where the Confederate Army of Tennessee of 38,000 men under General Bragg had been encamped for a month.

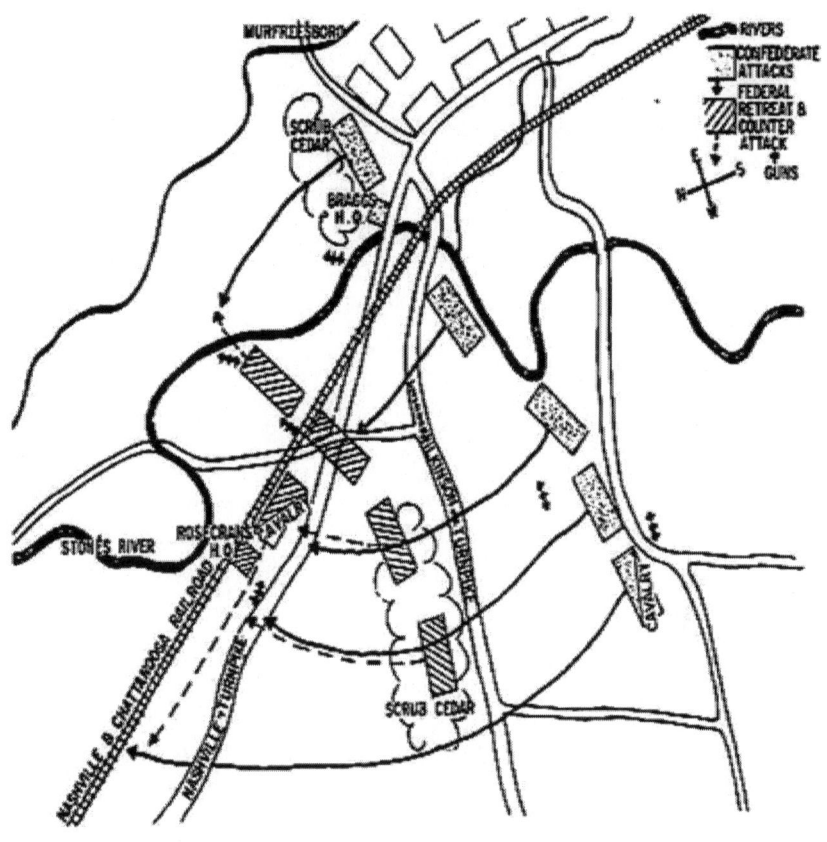

The battle of Murfreesboro, 1862

The Federal troops were in position by December 29th but made no attempt to launch an attack. At dawn on the 31st the rebels made a surprise attack on the Federal right flank and forced the Union line back so that by 10 a.m. it was at right angles to its original position. At the same time Confederate Cavalry made a bold sweep round the Federal forces and cut the railroad line in their rear. By n a.m. many of the Federal troops had begun to retire from lack of ammunition.

Rosecrans personally toured his hard-pressed lines, ordering his men to hang on with butt and bayonet if necessary, but he was unable to form up for a counter-attack. At dusk the fighting slowly came to an end.

Bragg expected the shattered Union army to withdraw and made no further moves. Rosecrans was, therefore, able to spend the whole of the next day in reorganising his forces. On January 2nd the Federal troops were still in position and Bragg ordered the division on his right flank to charge the Union lines—a charge of 500 yards across open ground.

Beyond the railroad signal box can be seen Colonel Hazen's artillery, the only Federal unit to hold its position during the fierce battle.

Murfreesboro reconstructed with Airfix figures. The Federal right flank has been pushed back and rebel cavalry are just cutting the railroad link to the Federal rear

Twenty minutes later the division retreated, leaving behind 1,800 men. Rosecrans had to pour reinforcements across the river but otherwise the charge had no effect.

That night Federal reinforcements began to arrive and Bragg was forced to retreat. Losses were over 25 per cent on each side: Union 13,000, Confederate 12,000.

American Civil War polystyrene figures by Britains in 54 mm scale

Fondouk, 1943

The Afrika Korps was retreating before the advance of the British Eighth Army when their rear was threatened by the British First Army advancing from the west. A small force of infantry was ordered to delay the British at Fondouk, a small gap in the hills.

This gap was a thousand yards wide with a dried up river bed running through it, dominated on both sides by rocky hills. The Germans dug in, backed in depth by numerous antitank guns and with wide minefields in front of them.

On the morning of April 8th British and American infantry attacked the hills on both flanks but were beaten back. A squadron of the 17/21st Lancers was ordered in to reconnoitre. Four tanks were lost in as many minutes and the squadron retired.

During the night the infantry tried again to dislodge the determined Germans but failed. The Welsh Guards were sent in to storm the hill on the left and they advanced stubbornly through a withering fire. They suffered some two hundred casualties, and failed. Time was now running out. General Crocker ordered the 26th Armoured Brigade to force the gap despite the fact that both flanks were still held.

The battle of Fondouk, 1943

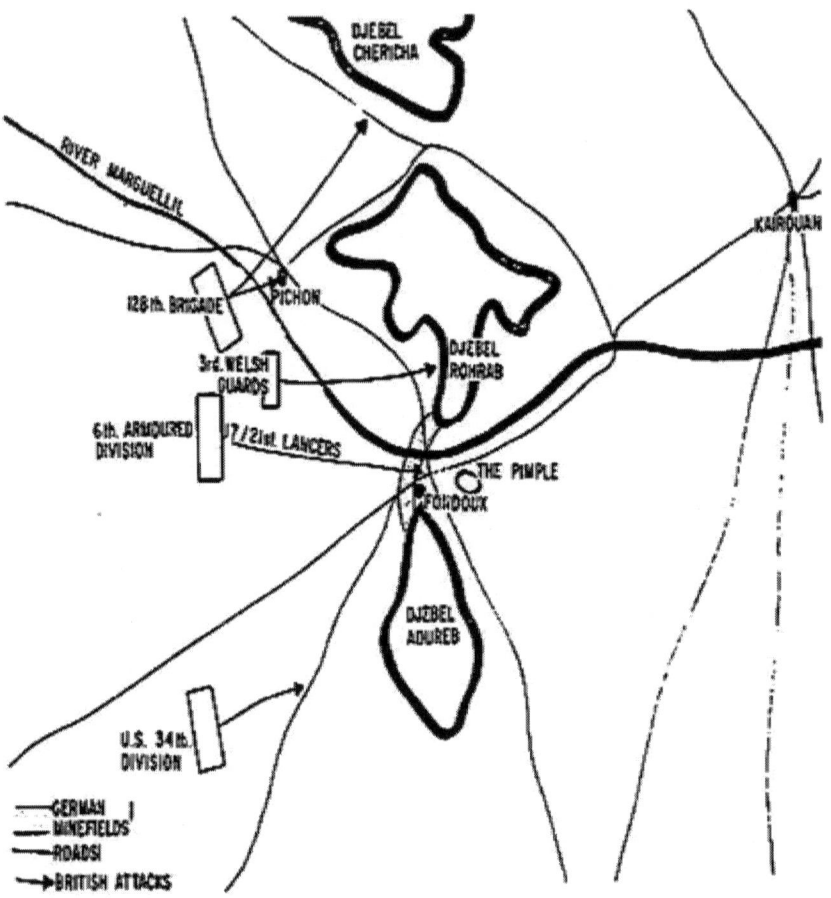

At 9 a.m. the 17/21st Lancers were again ordered in—this time to clear the pass regardless of cost. B squadron entered first.

There was no cover. Tanks soon began to grind to a halt as the 88s took their toll, aided by the mines which paralysed many other tanks. Machine guns and snipers took care of the crews as they baled out. Despite this one troop managed to break through, only to be destroyed by a nest of 88s concealed on the 'Pimple', an outcrop of rocks beyond the pass. Only two tanks survived out of the whole squadron.

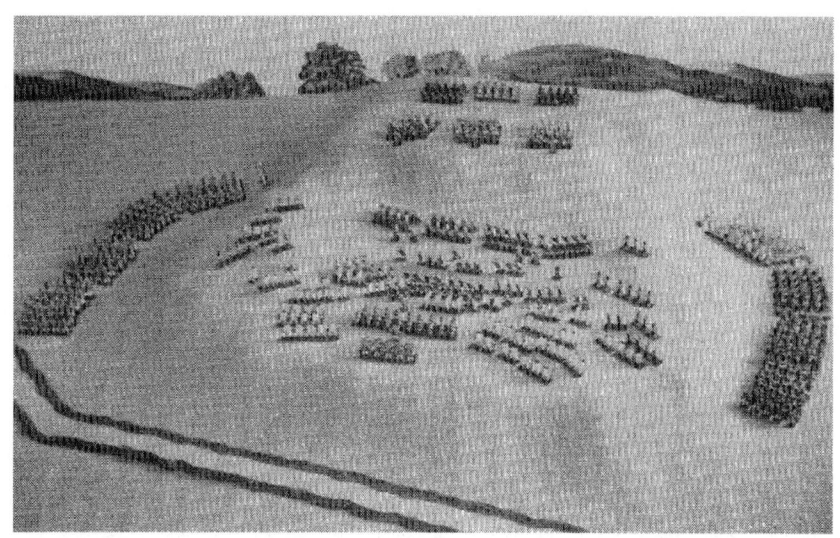

Above: A reconstruction for a wargame of the battle of Baecula, fought in Southern Spain between Rome and Carthage in 208 B.C. Two Roman columns are about to complete the classic pincer movement.

Another reconstruction, this time of the battle of Cross Keys, fought between Jackson's Army of the Valley and two divisions of Federal troops in 1862. Both photographs on this page are taken from books in the series Battles for Wargamers, by the author, which sets out to present wargamers with all the relevant facts and statistics so that they may refight actual battles.

The start of the battle of Bitter Creek, an 'imaginary' American Civil War battle fought by the author against one of his regular opponents.

The regiment that had charged the Russian guns at Balaclava had proved itself worthy of its noble tradition.

Close behind the shattered Lancers came the 16/5th Lancers and 2nd Lothians. Using a path cleared by the 17/21st the sister regiments penetrated the gap for the loss of another seven tanks. But the Germans had done their duty well. The tanks were too late to stop the Afrika Korps, which was streaming away northwards to fight yet another day. German losses were estimated at three tanks and 26 anti-tank guns.

Recruiting your army

Before any battles may be fought an army must be recruited and trained, exactly as in real life, and like a general you must choose the troops that will be best suited for the actions you have in mind.

Model soldiers come in a wide variety of sizes and prices. The sizes can be divided into three—54 mm, 30 mm and 20 mm, corresponding roughly to 2¼ in., 1¼ in. and ¾ in. All measurements are taken from the crown of the head, excluding the hat, to the top of the foot stand. The largest scale, 54 mm, is known to everyone, being the toy soldier of our childhood. These figures are really too large for battle gaming on a table top but they do have the advantage of being easy to handle and permit very fine detail of features and equipment.

This set of Airfix figures, which have been painted, can be used for many medieval periods with a little adaptation.

The 30 mm model is the original battle gaming size, though now overshadowed by the 20 mm. Again fine detail can be included on these models but, because they are not so popular nowadays, the range of accessories is limited. Between 30 mm and 20 mm is yet another scale—the 1 in. It is worth remembering that not all men are the same height and it is possible to use these 1 in. figures with 20 mm or 30 mm models—for instance, using the taller figures to form crack regiments of guards or grenadier companies

Lastly, the 20 mm range, the most popular battle gaming scale. (This is reflected in the huge range of tanks, guns, vehicles, aircraft, etc., that is available in the same scale.) Figures in this scale make even a small table seem enormous and permit reasonable numbers of vehicles and buildings to be used to create a realistic scene.

Figures in all these scales are available in either metal or plastic, both mediums having several advantages over each other. However, the biggest influence is the price and plastic is naturally much cheaper than metal.

Airfix 20 mm polystyrene figures. Sets such as this one of US Marines are very cheap.

25 mm mounted figures from the Les Higgins range painted and as supplied unpainted at right

30 mm metal figures by Allgeyer, about 1877

A selection of the excellent 20 mm metal figures made by Miniature Figurines

Solid and semi-solid elephant and camel corps figures by Allgeyer

Unpainted Hunt metal figures in 20mm scale. The same firm makes excellent 54mm figures.

A type of figure rarely mentioned these days is the 'flat' or profile figure. Mostly made in Germany the 'flats' were cut from sheets of lead and painted on both sides, normally in the 30 mm scale. All round, solid figures followed and in 1890 an Englishman named Britain discovered how to cast hollow soldiers. Since then 'flats' have largely disappeared from the everyday scene, though Donald Featherstone in his book *War Games* uses them to great effect to illustrate a battle set in ancient times.

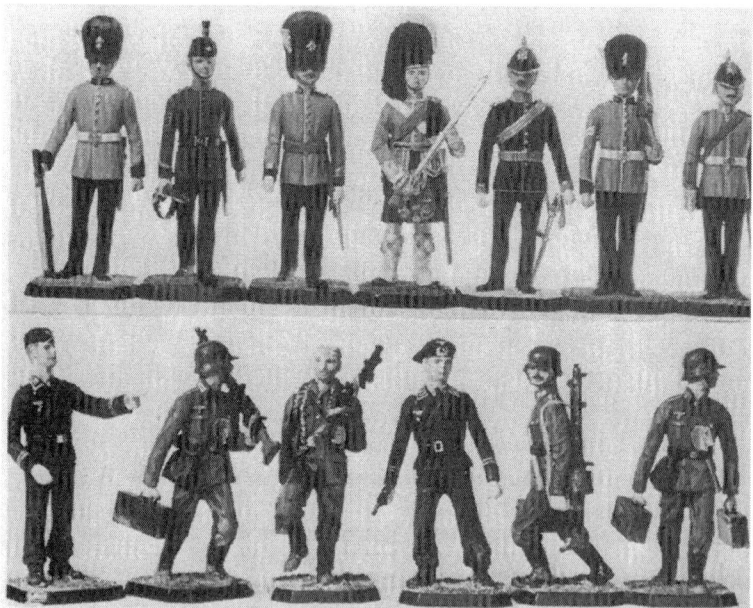

54 mm figures by Rose Miniatures who provide a vast range of figures to cover all phases of military history

Chapter 3 Basic Battlefield Layout

With the era and size of model decided on you now have only to choose your battlefield. Like most boys I played crude battle games on tables, floors and in the garden. The most satisfying medium was the garden, for, despite supervision, I managed to excavate trench systems in the rockery. Shell bursts were quite realistic, being simulated by a stick jabbed into the earth and jerked up, casting earth and bodies sky high at the expense of the flowers. But any collector of model soldiers will think twice before subjecting his troops to such conditions!

The earliest form of battle gaming. Castle and figures by Airfix

However, the basic principle of moulding real earth into a terrain is the Mecca of all battle gamers and is used by the armed services in the form of the sand table. This is a heavy, preferably metal table with a 6 in. raised edge all round. The table is covered with sand to a depth of 3 or 4 in. which can be moulded and coloured to produce any landscape required.

Such a table requires a spare room, the walls of which could be lined with maps, prints, weapons and shelves galore for the models when not in use. Unfortunately most of us have to make do with the living-room, and that only when no one else wants it. Dismiss the temptation to lay out your battle on the floor— not only do you get sore knees and an aching back but someone always manages to enter the room at a vital moment and tread on the forward positions.

Every battle gamer's dream! Veteran player Charles Grant discusses moves with his son in their battle gaming room [4].

The battleground

The battleground should be at table-top level, between 2½ and 3½ ft high—the higher the better. A cheap method of achieving this is to purchase a wallpaper table and two trestles, although this form of table does tend to wobble at the wrong moment. The simplest method is to use your existing dining table, extending its size by laying a large board on top of it.

Hardboard can be purchased in 6 ft x 4 ft, 8 ft x 4 ft or larger sizes but requires bracing with 2 in. x I in. or 6 in. x J in. prepared deal to prevent the corners drooping. If you use a glue such as Evostick, which makes a strong joint on impact 15 minutes after application, you can do away with unsightly nail heads. The bracing timber may be used either flat or standing on edge, the latter method giving more rigidity.

---

[4] His son was also called Charles Grant. The map being pointed to was their VFS/Lorrainne campaign map. A good number of the houses are still in use although the figures (Spencer Smith) are in semi-retirement now (in 2010) as brittle plastic has got the better of some. They have been replaced by Minden and RSM armies.

A dinner table quickly converted by covering with an old tablecloth. The hills are made from cushions, books and a pullover.

One method of stowing away such a board is to copy the model railway enthusiasts and hinge it to a wall so that it may be folded up or down when not in use and lay flush with the wall. This method is ideal for smaller boards, say 6 ft x 4 ft. If you fold the board up the battle gaming side is hidden and protected. Small boards such as this can do without a central brace and a wall map can be pasted on this reverse side, edged by battens that also act as bracing.

Board, 6 ft x 4 ft may sound a reasonably large board, and many players start with this size, but within three months it will seem tiny as the manoeuvres of the troops become more bold. Don't worry if this happens to you—if you start with a 12 ft x 8 ft board it will still seem too small eventually! The only sure way to decide on the .size of your board is to measure your room and see how big a board will fit in!

There are other limits. A width of over 5 ft makes it difficult to handle troops in the centre of the board unless you have exceptionally long arms. The length should be kept within a maximum of 10 to 12 ft otherwise you may find your troops so spread out that it takes half a day to perform a flanking movement.

A hardboard battle game board, fully dressed with accessories for a modern battle. Compare the effect of the background with the previous photograph

Stowage

With such large boards the problem of where to keep them becomes more acute. Many people in sheer desperation cut them in half and hinge the two parts together. This has its advantages, but it does create an unsightly crack right across the centre of the board. The only way to hide a large board intact is to make it part of the room.

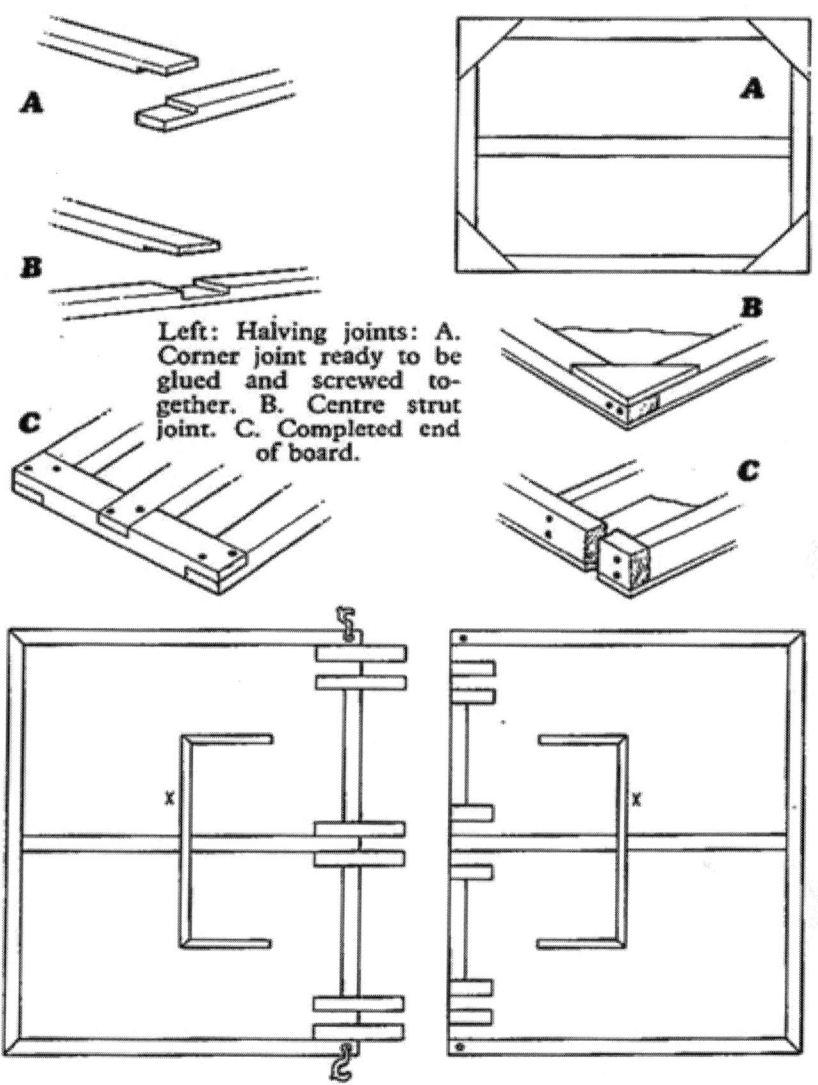

Left: Halving joints: A. Corner joint ready to be glued and screwed together. B. Centre strut joint. C. Completed end of board.

Top Right: Bracing the hardboard: in figures A and B the bracing is laid flat, strengthened at the corners with plywoood. In figure C it is used upright and an extra length fixed across the centre.

Bottom: An alternative to hinges, the two halves slotting into place. The two pieces marked X fit round the ends of the table to hold the board steady

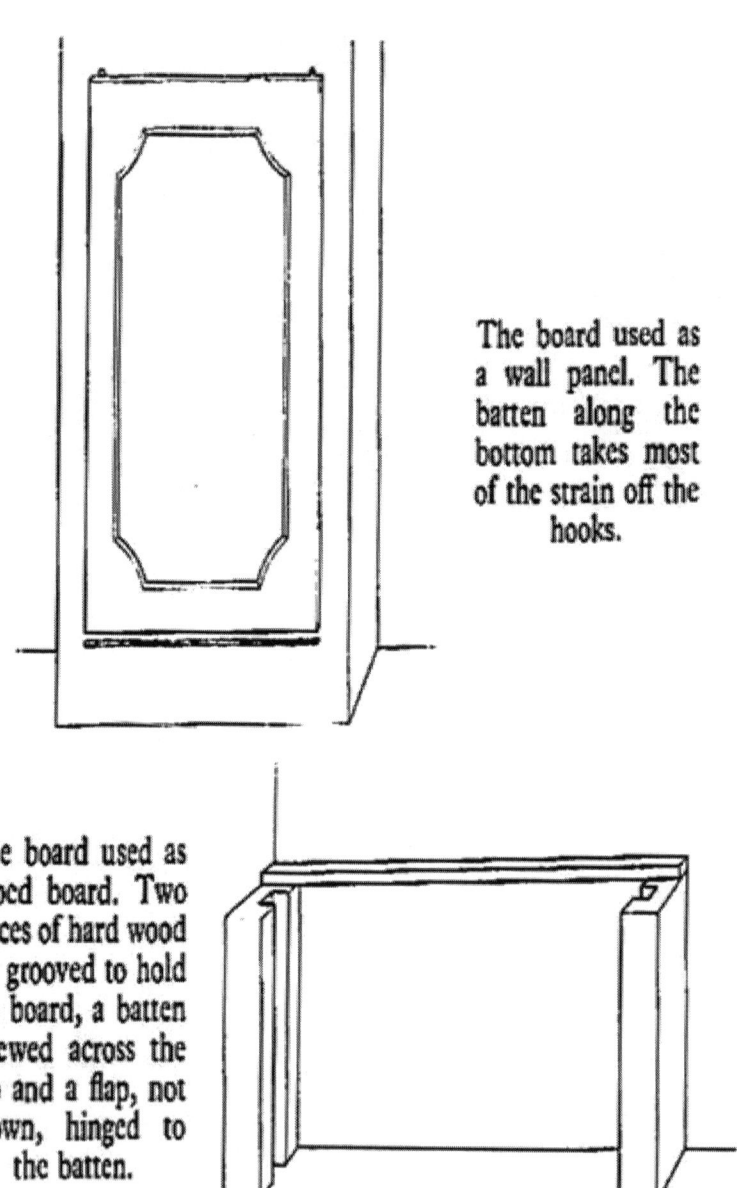

The board used as a wall panel. The batten along the bottom takes most of the strain off the hooks.

The board used as a bed board. Two pieces of hard wood are grooved to hold the board, a batten screwed across the top and a flap, not shown, hinged to the batten.

Four fields made from hardboard, rough side up. This shows how they break up the basic colour and flatness of the board.

Take your braced board and glue a second layer of hard-board on the reverse side. Paste wallpaper on this reverse side and add narrow beading, about 6 in. in from the edges, to break up the bareness. Set two hooks in the wall, screw two eyes to one end of the board and the whole thing can be hung on the wall in seconds to form an attractive panel. The ideal position is a chimney breast, especially if the fireplace is no longer used, but any large bare wall will do. A narrow batten along the line of tie bottom of the board will take a great deal of strain off the hooks and eyes. If the room being used is a bedroom use plastic quilting instead of wallpaper and place the board between bed and wall to protect the wall against damage.

A ploughed field made from corrugated cardboard. Walls by Bellona, fences by Airfix

Terrain

You will note that these suggestions assume that the board is totally flat whereas most landscapes have at least a few trees and hillocks. Model railway enthusiasts achieve quite fantastic masterpieces of miniature landscaping but, since no battle gamer wants to fight all his battles on the same terrain, in battle gaming all landscape features must be removable.

Paint your board a matt green—this will provide a base on which to build. I used emulsion paint since it dries quickly, the brush can be washed out in water and the finish is extremely tough. A pint will give you sufficient for two coats on a large board and still leave plenty for other items and for retouching the board at a later date.

Next make three or four small fields from squares of hard-board or corrugated cardboard. Be careful when cutting these since any lengths of wall or fence you buy will have to fit along the sides. If you use Airfix fencing for instance, which comes in 6 in. lengths, your fields must be 6 in. x 12 in., 12 in. x 12 in. or 6 in. x 18 in., allowing one side an extra inch or so for the gate. Paint these fields dark and light brown, yellow, or different shades of green. Place them on the board and you will see at once how they break up the basic colour and improve the appearance.

Hills

Now to arrange some movable contours. Hills have always been a major problem to battle gamers since they should appear realistic yet at the same time provide plenty of level spots for figures to stand on. There are several methods that can be used to produce suitable hills, all of them quite simple.

Mod-Roc is sold in the model shops and with this you can make a hill in under half an hour using only a bowl of water.

A packet of Mod-Roc contains strips of fabric impregnated with plaster of Paris which you dip in water and lay over a 'former' of crumpled newspaper, moulding it to the desired shape with your fingers. Decide roughly what your hill will look like before you wet the Mod-Roc—it sets in about 3 to 4 minutes and you need to work fast.

This method, though convenient, becomes expensive if you wish to make several hills. To make a hill from plaster of Paris you need only make a wooden base of the approximate size and shape of the intended hill. Mix the plaster on a plate and smear it over this 'former' with a knife. (When set the plaster can be broken off these tools quite easily.) I glued a sheet of stout cardboard to the base before applying the plaster and trimmed it off later. This prevents the hardened plaster from scratching the game board. Before the plaster sets—and you need to do this as soon as possible—scoop out one or two gun positions or trenches and make some small impressions with a flat-ended stick that will serve as standing positions for your figures.

Plaster of Paris takes a long time to dry out so leave the hill in a warm place for at least 24 hours. Then with an old penknife, level off more spots here and there, using a model figure to judge the base size correctly—they're bigger than you think. Finally, paint the hill with emulsion to match the board, using Humbrol matt 29 for earth where you have made emplacements. Humbrol matt 27 can be used for rocks or simply chip off pieces of plaster here and there to let the white plaster show through. Make sure when plastering that the edges come down flush with the board, avoid squarish shapes and you will find that these hills are quite realistic.

After painting the standing platforms can be seen more easily. Note how the top overhang provides cover for the gun and cover to hide two men or a machine gun underneath. Rocks have not yet been painted on.

An alternative method is papier mache. Use a wooden base as before, soak a pile of newspaper in water for about half an hour and make a cup of flour and water paste—using three desert-spoons of flour. Squeeze out the paper and place a layer over the wooden 'former'. Coat this with paste. Repeat this four or five times until you have built up sufficient thickness. Mould the paper into shape with your fingers, making level spots for the figures. Fold back any edges and press them into rock outcrops. Finally, coat the whole thing with a thick layer of paste to act as a seal and leave to dry in a warm place for about two days. The wooden 'former' can then be removed, or left in to act as a weight. Paint in the same manner as the plaster hill.

Rivers

Rivers add excitement to any battle game and are easily made from glass with a coat of paint on the bottom. However, this does get broken when packed away between games and a much more realistic product is marketed by Bellona in blue P.V.C. This comes in two widths, river or stream. I used the stream lengths, 20 in. for lap, since they were more to scale for my own layout. Apart from painting the banks these water sections need no other work. To add weight in order to prevent them slipping about, push plasticine into the hollows underneath the banks.

Roads

In all ages of warfare roads have played an important part and they are vital to battle gaming. To begin with I painted mine on the board, but despite its advantages this method soon cramps your imagination for layout schemes. The best method is to make the roads from a material that is smooth enough to stand figures on, yet is as thin as possible. I used cardboard, cut into 18 in. strips 2½ in. wide and painted with Humbrol matt 29. Unlike many other matt surfaces this has never flaked. White card is available from stationers, a huge piece costing about 10p being sufficient to produce enough roads, including bends and short end pieces, for any layout. Tuck each end slightly under the next to hold them in position and conceal the join.

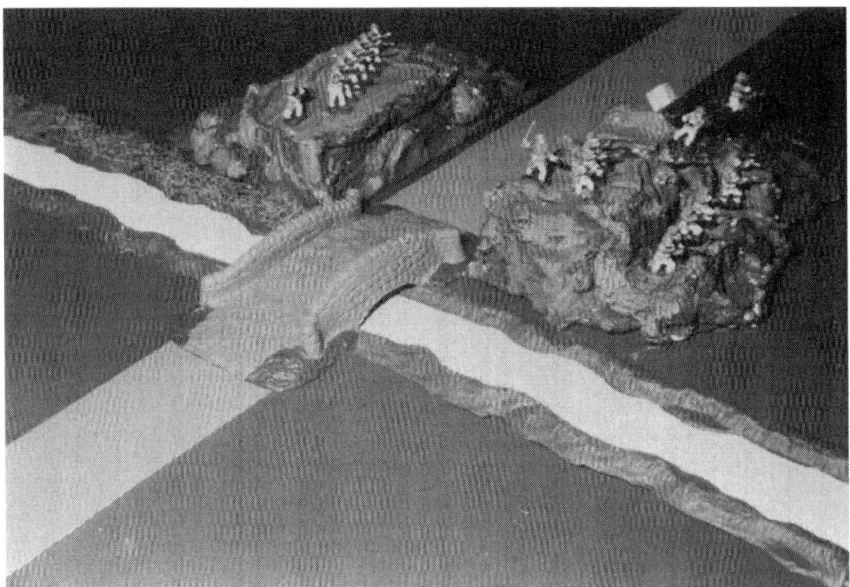

Stream lengths adapted for use with a Bellona bridge. The hills are plaster.

Federal troops using a road at the rear of their main position to rush reinforcements to the flank. A gun has half blocked the road causing some loss of speed- bad organization.

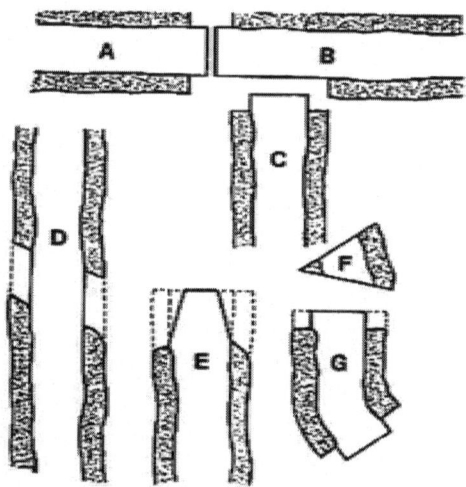

Bellona stream lengths showing adaptations. A and B a normal joint, B having one side cut back to allow for C which slots beneath the other two to form a T junction. D both banks cut to make a ford. E one end trimmed for insertion under a bridge. F and G short ends cut from a bend section to make gentle curves. Dotted lines show the original shape

Bellona stream lengths showing the overlapping joint, camouflaged with lichen and horsehair bushes. In the background Bellona's Menin Road diorama

Bellona also produce asphalt or concrete-textured sheets which can be used instead of cardboard, or the same firm's stream lengths can be painted brown and used as country lanes. They look better with lichen or foam rubber stuck along the tops of the banks and this will also provide cover for troops using the roads. Other methods include sandpaper or polystyrene sheet. Twenty thou, polystyrene sheet should be used since the thinner ones tend to curl up.

A ford—notice the abrupt river curves, the only ones available at present. The road is cardboard.

A German armoured car waits to dash across the board, using the road for maximum speed. The mere fact that it is in this position forces the other player to tie up men and equipment against a possible attack.

Tactical use of a layout

Once you have completed these pieces you have the basic layout for a battle game—the best battles do not necessarily take place on battlefields that are cluttered with fine examples of model making. The art of a good game is balance, balance between the two sides of the board, balance between open spaces and cover.

All troop movements on roads are increased by a bonus, i.e. if any infantryman moves 6 in. across a field he would move perhaps 8 in. along a road. By means of this bonus system the true value of roads in warfare is created. Most game boards are longer than they are wide, so when laying out your roads it is advisable to have one running the length of the board on each side, about a foot from the edge. These roads are soon in use for troop movement and immediately create the possibility of an attack to cut your opponent's supply line. Once cut, and with a strong body of men astride it, your opponent's communications between units are cut. A third road running across the board makes lightning attacks possible, especially by cavalry or vehicles moving at bonus rate. This causes the road to be heavily defended or even blocked by both sides, as often happens in real life. This road will also act as an approach road along which troops would move when first entering the battle.

In these two Civil War scenes the Federal troops (11th New York Zouaves) have managed to capture two hills and a bridge that were cleverly placed in the centre of the board. The rebels are now forced to make a costly assault in order to gain access across the river

When using a river in a layout bear in mind the number of bridges or fords you have available, for whilst rivers make good defensive positions they can be very difficult to cross when trying to launch an attack. Try to place the river in such a way that both players have equal advantage and disadvantage. The best way to achieve this is to place it roughly diagonally across the board or cross ways towards one end of the board so that it seals off one flank. The bridges then become extremely important and possession of them all could win the game.

Lastly, lay the hills on the board. It is important to remember that hills provide shelter for support troops, strong points for defence and advantages for artillery. If you have four hills, for instance, place one on each side to give equal shelter and gun positions but place the other two near the centre line and so cause a struggle for their possession.

In the central foreground is a young willow tree by Britains. On the extreme right a poplar tree by Merit. The round tree to the rear of the half track is made from a piece of sponge, 'careless' painting allowing the yellow of the material to show through and give a dappled effect.

Chapter 4 Adding Realism to your Layout

Most games for the Ancient or Horse and Musket eras can be played on a board such as was assembled in the last chapter but modern warfare normally requires a much more detailed layout. Also most players, having once collected their armies, turn to landscaping and try to add more and more realism to their battlefields. It is as well to remember one point—do not cram too much on a battlefield or you will ruin the game.

Trees and bushes

Some of the cover required for modern games can be quickly and cheaply produced from plastic foam. Bushes and hedges can be cut out with scissors quite easily, painted in matt colours and be in use in a few hours. Trees improve a layout considerably and can also be made from plastic foam with a round lolly stick for a trunk. Other methods are to make wire frames and stick on to them flock or lichen, or cardboard profiles can be cut out and glued to a wooden base. Most model firms produce fine plastic trees but they are usually rather expensive.

Bridges and fencing

If you are using a river on your layout you will soon find that you never seem to have enough bridges! You can make one from a piece of balsa wood, some cardboard or polystyrene sheet and some brick or stone paper. The same applies to fencing and walls, although in this case most firms manufacture them so cheaply and the detail is so tine that it is usually better to buy than make. Airfix and Gem (from Beatties) both do excellent fencing at very cheap prices but they need to.be glued to the roads for best effect as they are really designed for model railways. Bellona make superb walls that can be fitted in anywhere, so the answer is to have some lengths of road without fencing and others with the fencing glued on. If you use these in the right places, and plan beforehand how to use your wall sections and gates, you will be able to have both good defensive cover and realism.

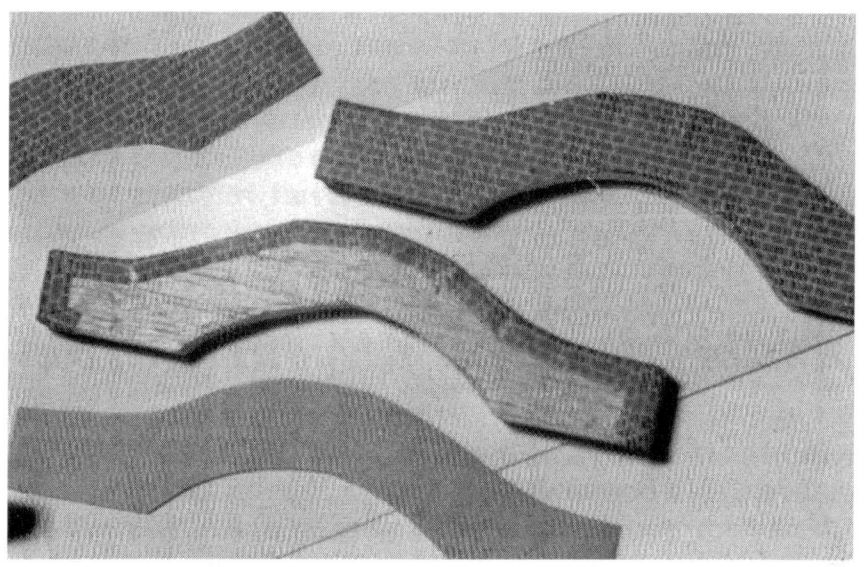

Two balsa wood 'knees' with brick paper and a strip of polystyrene are all that are needed to make your own bridge.

To make the polystyrene stay in this humped shape use a fair amount of cement, hold it in position for three minutes and allow to set overnight. The assault gun is an Airfix kit

Britains' 54 mm trees

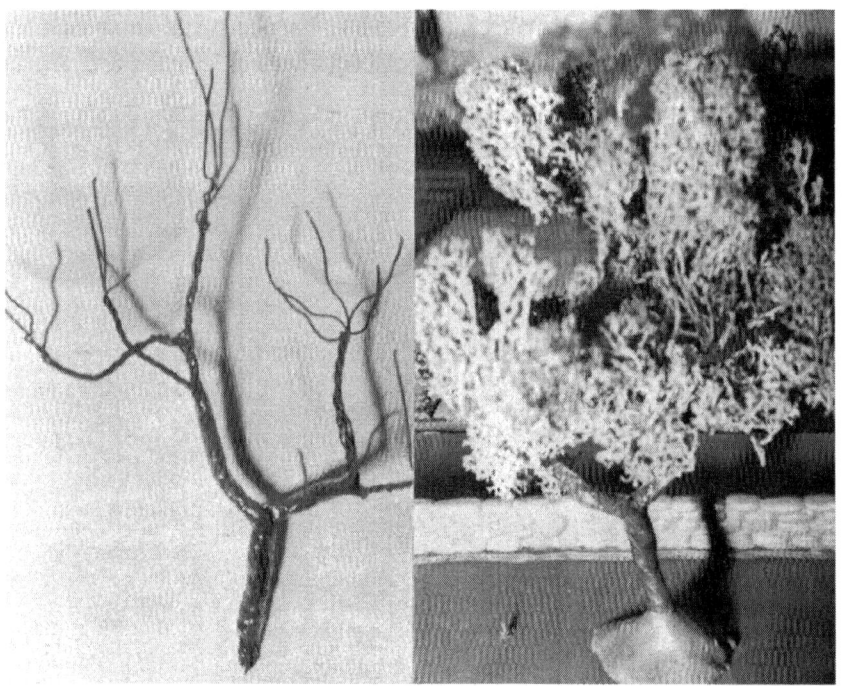

Left: Lengths of copper wire twisted together to form a tree. Right: Trunk has been painted and stuck into a Plasticene base. Lichen is glued to the branches

Finishing touches to the landscape can be obtained free from your garden. Large stones make better rocks than any plastic ones and a few twigs make excellent fallen trees or piles of timber, ideal for gun positions. Other accessories, such as broken wagons, water pumps, troughs and animals, can be added and do create a realistic scene, but personally I find they get in the way of the important figures.

Buildings

An odd building or two will improve any layout and you will no doubt eventually end up with a whole town at your disposal. There is a wide selection of buildings on the market and it is best to consider them all carefully before starting your collection.

Many simple buildings can be made from cardboard, glue, Sellotape and brick paper and a solid if unimaginative building can be made from a block of wood. There are now many manufacturers of cardboard buildings and the detail on these products is so perfect that it is hardly worth while making your own.

Minitanks' fir trees. Each tree is in 8 pieces but can be arranged, as shown here, to give different sizes

My own equipment is all packed away at the end of each game and after a time I find that cardboard buildings begin to get ragged at the edges. Most of the plastic buildings on the market can be used for the seventeenth century onwards, some of the farmhouses being quite all right for earlier battles too. The Airfix kits are especially good since the roofs can be left unattached and the interior of the buildings used. I find it convenient to leave the building in two halves also, front and one side, back and other side, so that the model figures can be placed inside the building more easily and, if the building should be destroyed, part of it can be removed to show this.

Small twigs from the garden take on the appearance of tree trunks when used with 20 mm figures. The farmhouse is an Airfix kit.

A small village is being used here to launch an assault. The buildings can be used to build up small forces who then leap-frog from house

Opposite arc examples of houses made from card. *Left:* A and B: Corrugated card for log cabins with twigs at corners and door. C and D: Card strips cut to represent tiles. *Right:* A: Fold along all lines and glue, making a box. B: Cut off four corner sections, fold along dotted lines, glue A over B and C over D. C: The completed sections. *Bottom:* A: Cut all continuous lines, fold along broken lines and C-D. B: Glue A over B. C: Glue E over F. D: An extra piece forms the roof overlap.

Uses of cover

Having spent many hours constructing all this equipment it is important that you lay out your battlefield in such a way that you obtain the most use and enjoyment from it—there is little fun in making a bridge if it never comes under attack and remains unused throughout the game.

Two machine guns, a, tank and supporting infantry make full use of the cover provided by this hill to guard a vital crossroads in the rear. The plaster hill was made especially to fit crossroads such as this

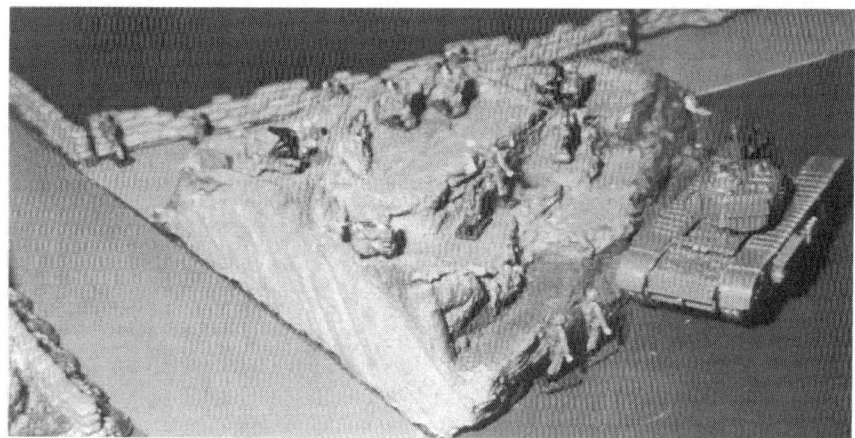

Always avoid having large empty spaces in your layout since a player has only to advance across an open field once in his life to learn that he must never do it again! As in real warfare the casualties from artillery and infantry fire make it hardly worth while unless his opponent can be caught unawares. Usually if there is a big field on the layout no one will venture near it and that part of the board becomes completely dead. If you do have a big field you can fill it with buildings but remember this will almost certainly become the scene of much hand-to-hand fighting, so leave a reasonable amount of room between houses.

In smaller open spaces place farmhouses, barns, haystacks, a few rocks or a pile of tree trunks. This enables a player to cross the field in short hops—a tactic that can often only be stopped by a bayonet charge! Also a player may build up a considerable force under cover, then suddenly charge out to attack.

To create shelter for reserves to the rear, place your trees in an outline of a wood, leaving the centre empty. Troops may then be moved in or out without having to constantly move trees out of the way. Odd trees can be placed as road blocks, but remember that your own troops can't fly and don't block a road you may want to use later.

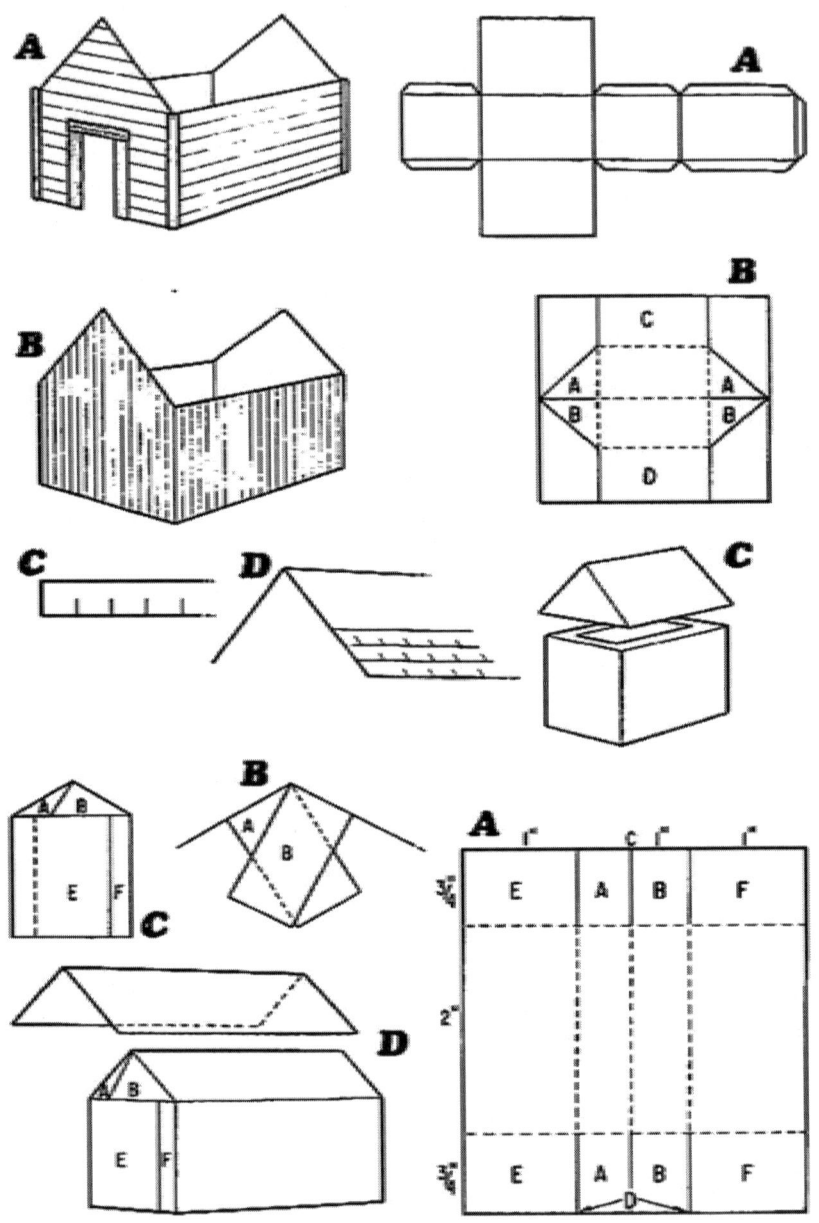

Use your walls and fencing to seal off fields as in real life but be careful where you place the gates. It is all very well to send trucks or wagons haring along a road at the bonus rate, but useless if you discover too late that there is no gate to get into that part of the field! Be sure to leave gates and roads free of obstructions.

Your battlefield is now set. Maybe you have set it out yourself, or your opponent, or both of you together. It doesn't really matter who lays it—though it is fun to work it out together—so long as you strive to make the advantages and disadvantages as equal as possible. That you will do so is decided by a rule: both players toss a dice, the highest score having the advantage of choosing from which side of the board to fight.

Chapter 5 Organising your Army

Although everything now appears to be set for battle there is still an important factor missing. This is the organisation of your army, a factor that may go a long way towards giving you victory or defeat.

The basic organisation of armies has altered considerably over the years, not so much because of new tactics but because of new weapons. The Greeks invented the phalanx, which was in fact a mobile hedgehog of spear points. Elephants, chariots and cavalry were employed to soften it up. The Romans invented conscription to ensure a constant supply of trained men: also they split the mass of men common in Ancient warefare into maniples or literally 'handfuls' of men, who could be more easily controlled and manoeuvred. Hannibal used cavalry to smash the legions and later the barbaric hordes from Asia swept all before them, mounted on hardy ponies. The stirrup was invented, giving horsemen much more control over their mounts and enabling them to fight more efficiently: gradually the cavalry began to take precedence over the infantry.

A Roman cohort opening its ranks to allow elephants to pass through. The main purpose of these fighting animals was to break up solid formations.

A few knights and a handful of trained men-at-arms inside a castle could hold off rebels for months. Here professional soldiers and peasants are attacking. The archers, who are giving covering fire, are using mobile shields for protection.

An assault tower in use during a siege. From the top: archers forcing the men on the ramparts to stay under cover, swordsmen ready to charge across the ramp, a ram for battering down the wall if the attack on top fails.

Army Organisation

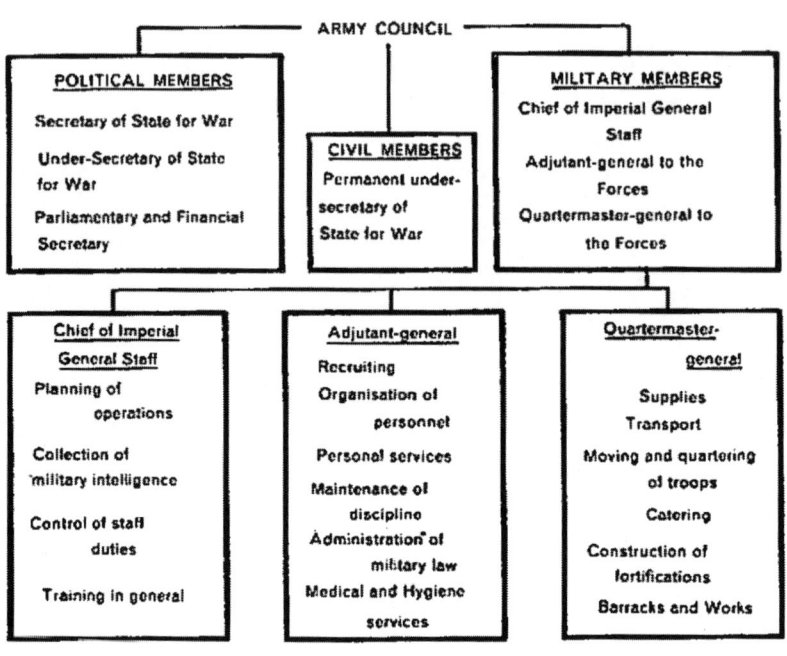

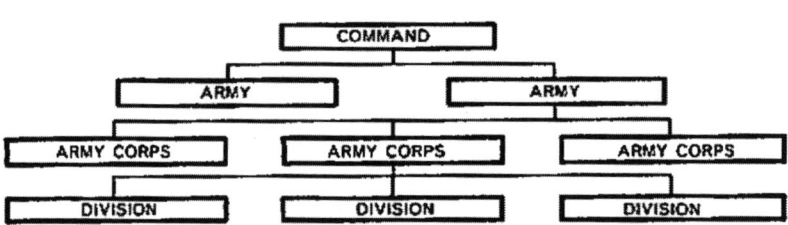

Top level British Army organisaton at the outbreak of the Second World War

The armour worn by cavalry began to increase in quantity and thickness until, over the centuries, the infantry disappeared entirely from the scene—except for peasants who were raised in emergencies. At Agincourt the French had 24,000 men, almost all knights, and the common soldier was so insignificant that he was not even included amongst the casualties. This opinion was reversed by the English archers, the French nobles eventually considering it an honour to serve as an archer! The archers were used to counter heavy cavalry charges and organised infantry was reintroduced to protect the archers. In the early fourteenth century the Swiss 'discovered' the phalanx and armed with the pike dominated European wars until the invention of gunpowder.

Cavalry were rendered impotent by the arquebuses of the infantry and they were relegated to reconnaissance work or acting as mounted infantry. Pikemen were used in a ratio of two to one at this time to protect the arquebusiers while they reloaded. About this time the formation known as a regiment came into use, and fater the formation of divisions.

The famous British square, a defence formation that was rarely broken. A cannon is mounted at each corner, cavalry would normally be in the centre of the square.

German infantry using their supporting tanks for cover. Eventually tanks had a telephone on the rear to give communication between tank commander and infantry officers.

An Army Division

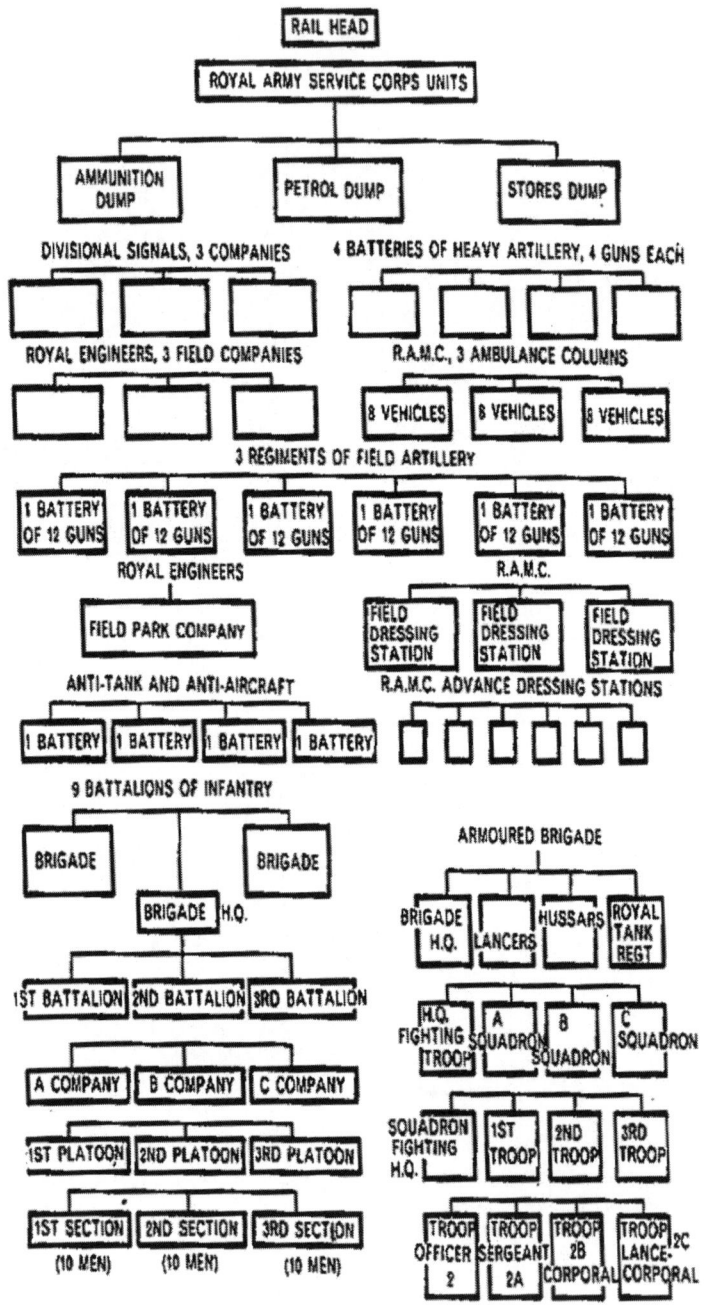

A British division of 1936. Notice there are 9 battalions of infantry to 3 regiments of tanks

When bayonets were invented each arquebusier became his own pikeman and about the same time the cavalry began to come to the fore again, charging to the attack between volleys. The French started using peasant irregulars as skirmishers in force, backed up by regulars in column. Using the famous thin line Wellington often caught the French in this formation

Confederate cavalry charging round the Federal flank. In the American Civil War most cavalry fought as mounted infantry and was able to pour terrific musket fire on the head and flanks of the columns before they could deploy.

Most major powers experienced colonial wars in the latter half of the nineteenth century and this more than anything else led to the abandoning of massed formations. The breech-loading rifle forced the cavalry, unable to press home a charge against such firepower, to revert to mounted infantry and scouts again. The use of railways, machine guns, trenches, gas, tanks and aeroplanes followed in swift succession to give us the type of warfare well known in the twentieth century.

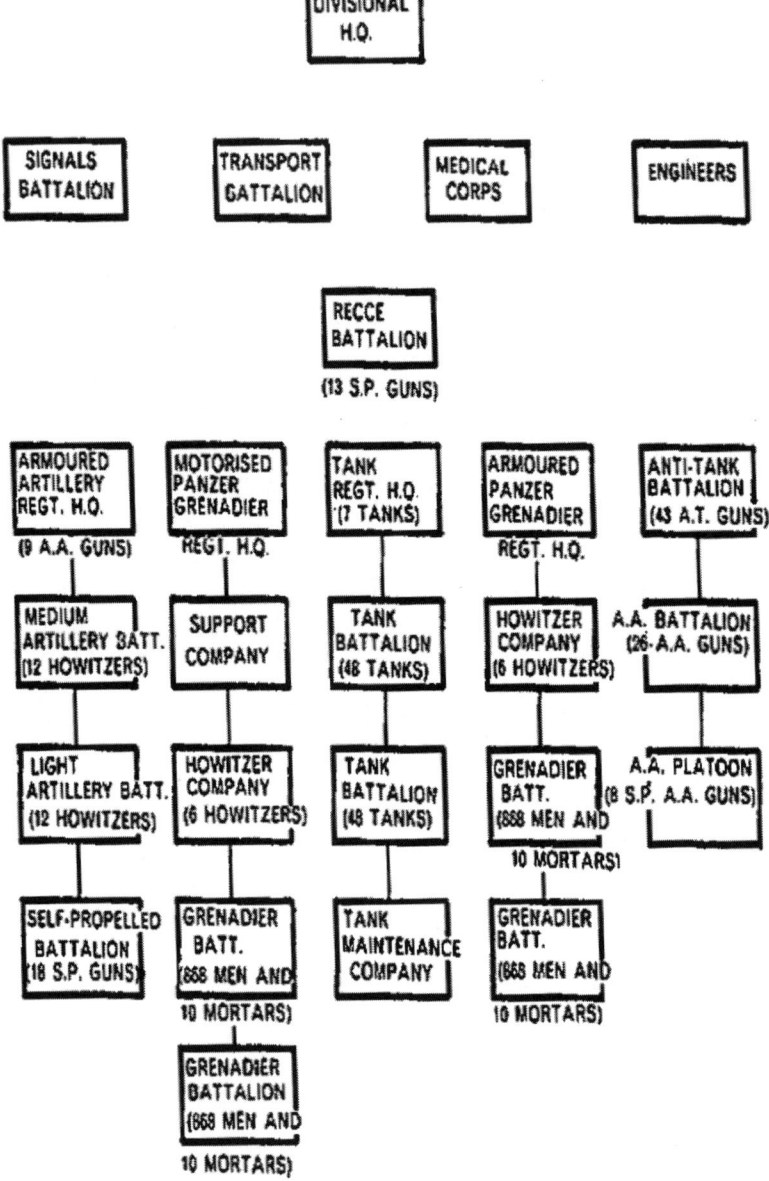

A German Panzer division of 1943 with 2 tank battalions, 1 anti tank and 1 S.P. battalion to 6 motorised infantry battalions.

Basic formations

From all of this can be seen that the organisation of a Roman legion with perhaps 6,000 infantry and only 300 cavalry is far different to the

Royalist Army during the English Civil War when cavalry often outnumbered infantry. These facts should be taken into consideration when buying your troops.

However, I have found that too many artillery or cavalry tend to cause casualties out of all proportion to reality and it is, therefore, advisable to consider not only the historical facts but also the realities of the gaming board.

The Roman legion of about 100 B.C. usually consisted of 6,000 infantry in 10 cohorts with 300 cavalry, supported by auxiliary archers. If one model figure equals 20 you have a legion of 300 infantry, 15 cavalry and some 30 auxiliaries. The legion is opposed by a mass of 'barbarians' in overwhelming numbers because the Roman figures have the advantage of armour and shields.

In the modern era I use three sections of infantry, 10 men to a section, as the basic unit. They can operate as three sections of a platoon, or three platoons of a company, or three companies of a battalion. Formation of a weapons platoon with machine guns and mortars offers scope for the players with a flair for conversion. The artillery and tanks need to be kept low. With each 100 infantry I have a battery of three field guns or howitzers, three anti-tank guns and a troop of three or four tanks.

For the American Civil War I use a brigade of 81 infantry (three regiments of 27 men each) backed by a battery of three guns and a squadron of cavalry—13 men.

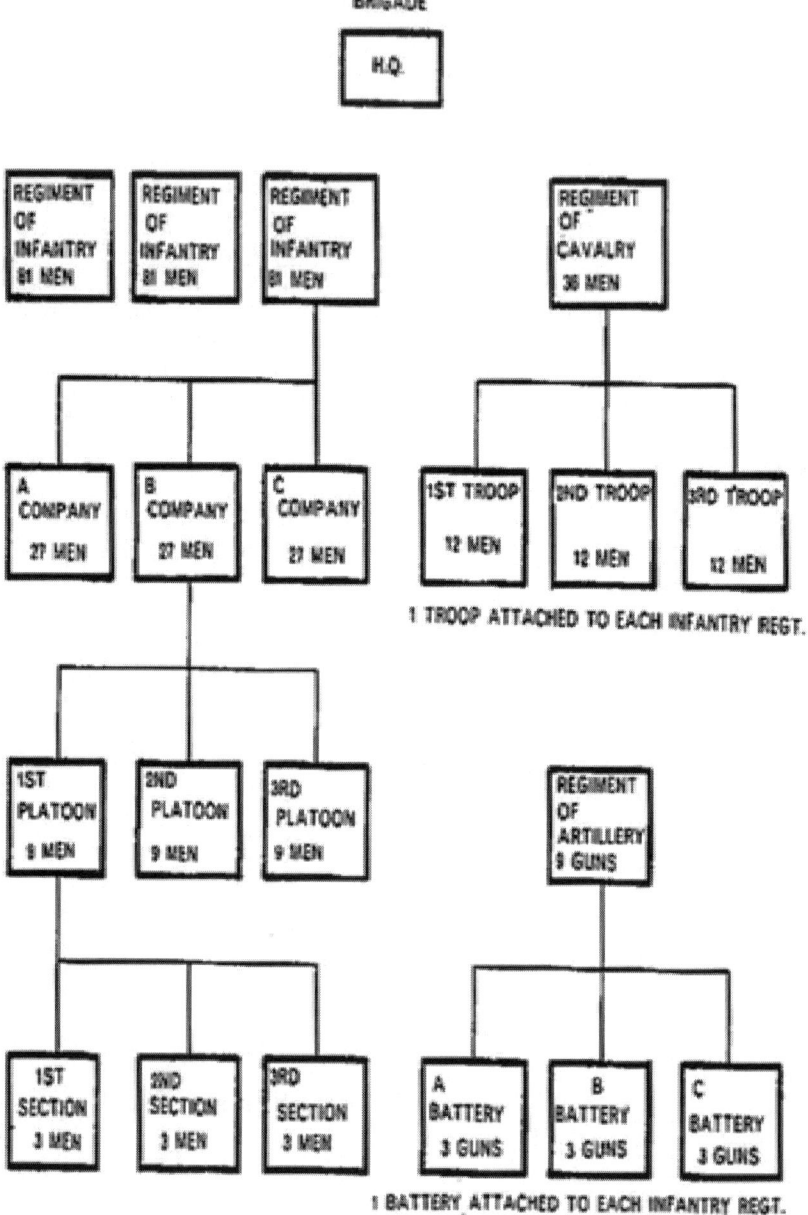

Suggested organisation for a model army, covering the period 1850 to 1945. Cavalry would be replaced by 3 tanks per troop.

Uses of the different arms

Players should use their own discretion when laying troops on a board and never stick to strict regimentation. For instance, a player with three squadrons of cavalry, each attached to a brigade of infantry, could group the cavalry into a brigade. He would lose cavalry support with each brigade of infantry but gain a mounted force that could hit hard and fast. However, such a large body of mounted men is hard to keep under cover and draws heavy artillery lire so that often it suffers heavy losses before coming into action. Also the other player will often mass his own cavalry to meet his opponent's force head on. There follows a short but glorious cavalry battle, leaving the remainder of the game without that spice of danger that only the threat of a cavalry charge can add.

It is also possible to concentrate your artillery in the same way, but this turns into an artillery duel when your opponent does the same, both sides merely striving to destroy each other's guns and crews.

It is best, therefore, to keep your forces in a formation that enables each part of the line to have support from each arm. Guns or cavalry can always be moved from point to point as required later in the game.

Ancient figures from Sheriff of Nottingham and Robin Hood sets. Bill-hook man reduced to a swordsman; man-at-arms with shield added; archer with sword and shield replacing his bow; man-at-arms with axe painted to resemble a peasant or Viking; another bill-hook man with shield added and a bowman converted by adding shield and sword.

Roman auxiliaries from the Airfix Indian set. The two horsemen on the left have had their rifles replaced by swords made from the ends of pins; the one on the right has had his headdress trimmed off.

Machine gun teams from basic figures: the British gunner (left) was a wireless operator, the German held a sub-machine gun.

American Civil War figures made from the Cowboys set.

Airfix Roman figures. The two charioteers—plumed helmets—have had shields and bases added to become centurions; the centurion has lost his helmet plume and been given a shield of polystyrene.

However, there is always the exception to the rule. If at the start of a game you see a physical feature that will enable you to gain an advantage, by all means concentrate troops and guns here—but remember your opponent may be doing the same.

Rules of the game

Everything is now ready to begin, except for the rules of the game. Depending on an agreement between players a game may be started by laying all your pieces on the edge of the board behind a start line, 9 in. or a foot from the edge of the board, or by moving them on to the board unit by unit as the game progresses, arriving on the scene along one or two approach roads.

The vital decision of where to deploy your troops at the beginning of a game, perhaps concentrating in one place at the expense of weakening another part of your line, can be very difficult—but that is a commander's job, and in battle gaming *you* are the general!

The rules that appear in the next three chapters are not official rules, nor are they complete: they are intended to serve only as a basis to guide the newcomer to battle gaming. The rules I first used were 'invented' before I even knew what the game was called. A nephew had some Airfix figures, I was a keen amateur photographer and from table-top photography developed a game. Those initial rules were later influenced by Donald Featherstone, whose book in turn introduced me to H. G. Wells. Later still my rules became totally altered by 'wartime' experience and with each new book or fresh magazine article I read the rules change and improve.

British troops of the late nineteenth century. From the left: Federal trooper painted black and green for light infantry; three First World War Germans painted as men of a line regiment; Civil War artillery man painted to represent their officer; a German figure converted to a standard bearer; mounted artillery figure painted to represent a light infantry officer; the next three figures, taken from Federal troops, are painted for light infantry; the Guards officer at the end was a trumpet player in the band before promotion.

By some uncanny sense H. G. Wells realised that battle gamers are all great individualists, strongly opposed to the regimentation they demand of their troops. He set out a list of undeveloped ideas and left each battle gamer to adapt them to suit his own personality. (Some players mercilessly kill all their opponent's men, some have wounded men, some are even so humane as to take prisoners!)

The rules listed here are for you to try out. Adjust the ideas to suit yourself, reject or accept them as you please. The establishing of rules is as much a part of the hobby as building an army. Once you have mastered these basic ideas there are other books and several sets of rules available that give precise rules to cover all conceivable events that might happen in a battle.

A Roman legion in battle formation: 1st line, auxiliary skirmishers to break up enemy attacks and preserve the legionnaires' tight shield line, 2nd line, young men with no battle experience.' 3rd line', experienced men. 4th line, veterans who would only fight as a last resort or could be used in a flanking attack. There are a few auxiliary cavalry on each wing.

Chapter 6 The Rules for Ancient Warfare

The rules for battle games vary considerably with the era in which the battles are being fought, and for this reason a chapter has been devoted to each of the major periods: Ancient, Horse and Musket and Modern in that order.

Most battles in ancient times took place in a small area with the opposing armies in full view of each other. This helps to make ancient battles realistic even on a small board and also enables relatively straightforward rules to be used. Rules can be divided into three main parts: Movement, Firing and Mêlées. We will deal with movement in ancient times first, but a few preliminary words are necessary to explain the reasons for some general rules.

In battle gaming tactics are vital but there is also the element of luck. Where possible the rules are designed to give advantage to the player using the best tactics, but luck has been allowed a small part so that it is possible for sudden, unaccountable reversal to take place as in actual warfare. The throw of a dice represents luck and because of this the use of dice has been kept to a minimum

Methods of moving

Originally moves were always taken alternately, as in almost all board games, but simultaneous moves are becoming popular. In the alternate method the player to move second has the advantage of seeing his opponent's initial move, but when the second player makes his move *his* opponent can then see what move to make in retaliation. This continues throughout the game and probably evens out in the long run. This is the method described in the rules in this book.

For those wishing to use the simultaneous move, which is after all the more realistic, there is only one extra task. Before each move the players write down what moves they intend to make. These written orders are then placed in full view and both players make the moves described. This enables both sides to move at once without a player, who suddenly sees a threat developing, being able to change his mind in mid-move!

It remains now only to decide what distance the different pieces may cover on each move. If an infantryman covers 6 in. each move then a cavalryman would be expected to move twice as fast while a heavy, wheeled vehicle would move at half the pace. This gives a simple scale:

Infantry, wagons and elephants, 6 in.
Chariots, cavalry and staff officers, 12 in.
War engines on wheels, 3 in.

Ballista made by Britains in the 54 mm scale

All pieces moving along roads would have the distance covered increased by a third.

Movement rules

All moves are measured from the leading figure and players may only measure distances when actually making their move.

Measuring at any other time is forbidden. (Judging distances for counter-attacks must be done by eye!)

A dice is thrown to decide which player will move first. He moves his pieces as desired but no firing may take place. The other player then moves his pieces. The first player makes his second move, ending the move with Firing and the game continues with alternate moves, each move being terminated by Firing. The vital rule here is that Movement always precedes Firing.

Between moves some players are inclined to ponder at great length on their next move, especially if they are losing! A time limit of three minutes has been imposed between the last move of one player and the first move of his opponent to prevent the game 'bogging down'.

War engines take one move to ascend or descend a hill and may only cross rivers by bridges. If their crews are killed other figures may be moved up to replace them.

Airfix Arabs, also useful for this era. The camel men make Bactrian camel cavalry

Chariots may only cross rivers by bridges or fords. Elephants may cross anywhere but have their move reduced by half unless using a bridge or ford.

Cavalry and infantry may cross a river anywhere but their move is reduced by half unless they use a bridge or ford. They may pass over fences and walls without hindrance unless confronted by, a wall higher than 1 in. Infantry may climb this but their move is reduced by half.

Cavalry and infantry must be led by an officer when advancing. (More experienced players use a set of morale rules. This simple rule replaces them.) If infantry lose all their officers whilst advancing they must be turned to face the rear and retreat on their next move. They must continue to retreat until another officer arrives to lead them. Once a cavalry charge has begun it cannot be halted by the loss of officers. However, if they are not charging when the officers are lost they must turn and retreat on the next move, continuing to retreat until an officer arrives to lead them.

If retreating infantry are forced into a river, except at a ford, they lose one-third of their number in crossing.

No form of artillery may move *and fire,* but it is expected that legionnaires with pilum could discharge their weapons on the move, as could archers who would also be able to reload on the move. Therefore, all cavalry and infantry, including chariots and elephants, are capable of firing *and moving.*

Firing rules

Since we are working on a 6 in. infantry move, artillery should be capable of reaching targets within 2 ft of their position, a bow and arrow would reach 12 in., spears and stones from slings 6 in. Boulders used in defence of a castle may only be dropped on figures immediately below the apertures.

Firing takes place at the end of each move, except the opening move. The men killed by the first player should be left lying on the board until the second player has finished his firing so that he may include them. With the simultaneous move firing also takes place simultaneously and it works best if the players begin on one flank and work systematically across the board.

Archers and slingers may fire from any position but spearmen may only discharge their weapon if they are in the front rank. Spearmen may only fire once in a game. (In fact the opposing armies relied on each other's volleys of spears for ammunition—hence the Roman pilum which was designed to snap off at the" head and rob the enemy of ammunition!)

20 mm scaling ladders made from four matchsticks and some slivers of polystyrene, stuck together with polystyrene cement.

A simple howdah made from plastic card. Two archers fit in comfortably without trimming their bases. A third will go in at a pinch. The howdah is secured with ribbon, fastened with Uhu glue.

For each ten men firing throw one dice. The score indicates the casualties inflicted. If there is an odd number of men, such as 35, a dice is thrown for the five and the score halved. Fractions under five do not receive a dice throw.

If the men being fired on are bearing shields, in chariots or elephant howdahs, crews of war engines, or are under cover of walls, buildings, etc., then the casualties are halved. Cavalrymen count as two points, needing a throw of two to remove a man and his mount.

Mobile ram made from a sharpened twig, the wheels made from balsa wood and fastened on with pins.

Elephants from Britains. The baby is just right for a 20 mm war elephant. Cut the ridged spine above the back legs and level off the back to take a howdah (opposite).

Every six that is thrown removes an officer, or if no officer is available, the normal six men. If two sixes are thrown an officer of staff rank may be removed if in range: if three sixes are thrown the commanding general may be removed if in range.

When firing on chariots or elephants a player has two alternatives. He may scatter his fire amongst them and take casualties from all the pieces or he may concentrate on a few. He must state his intentions before firing. By concentrating on two or three chariots, for example, he could kill all the men in them and so put them out of action. He could, however, throw a high score and waste points.

Chariots that have been emptied by enemy fire continue to advance in the direction they were pointing. Whichever side reaches them first may re-man them. Elephants that lose their crews also continue in the direction they were pointing but become uncontrollable. At the end of each move a dice must be thrown to see which direction they will point prior to moving again; six or five continue ahead, one or two turn to face the opposite direction, three turn left and four turn right. Any infantry in their path during these stampedes are removed.

A player trying to kill an elephant must state his intention before firing and must score a six to succeed. The crew are not killed.

Each war engine uses two dice when firing. Two sixes kills an elephant and crew or destroys a chariot and crew or destroys another war engine and crew. Infantry and cavalry casualties are at the normal rates.

Mêlée Rules

When troops become involved in hand-to-hand fighting luck begins to crop up. In real life individual soldiers possess different ability in hand-to-hand combat and it is unrealistic to line 20 men against 30 and expect the numerically superior force to win every time. Therefore, all mêlées are ruled by the throw of the dice. More humane players long ago realised that it was not right to slaughter all opposing troops and arrangements have been included for the taking of prisoners, though I must admit I never seem to have many!

Directly opposing forces come into actual contact, or within ½ in. of each other, a mêlée takes place and must be fought after the movement and firing has been completed.

Artillery or infantry on the nearby flanks may not fire into the mêlée because of the danger to their own men. The pieces involved in the mêlée are determined before the dice are thrown. All troops within a 6 in. radius of the point of impact are included: other pieces outside this area may move up on the next move to be included in a renewed or extended mêlée.

Starting with the player who moved his pieces into contact, each player throws a dice four times and removes from the board the number of men indicated by the dice. A six takes an officer, two consecutive sixes a staff officer if available. When officers arc not available the normal number of men are taken. If one side is totally removed before or by the end of the four throws then he has naturally lost the mêlée. If any officers are left they must fall back on the nearest friendly troops within range. If there are no friendly troops within range then the officers are captured.

By the end of four throws there will be a gap between the opposing forces, enabling the mêlée to be broken off by either side on the next move, or to be renewed. This method also enables support troops to be brought up if a player decides to extend a mêlée into a major action.

An assault tower, a useful accessory in medieval games, made from a frame of 1/8 in. balsa and plastic card. It is not tall enough to reach the towers but the ramp will lay across the walls.

The assault tower under construction. Blocks and cleats were taken from a ship kit, the ramp was hinged with Sellotape

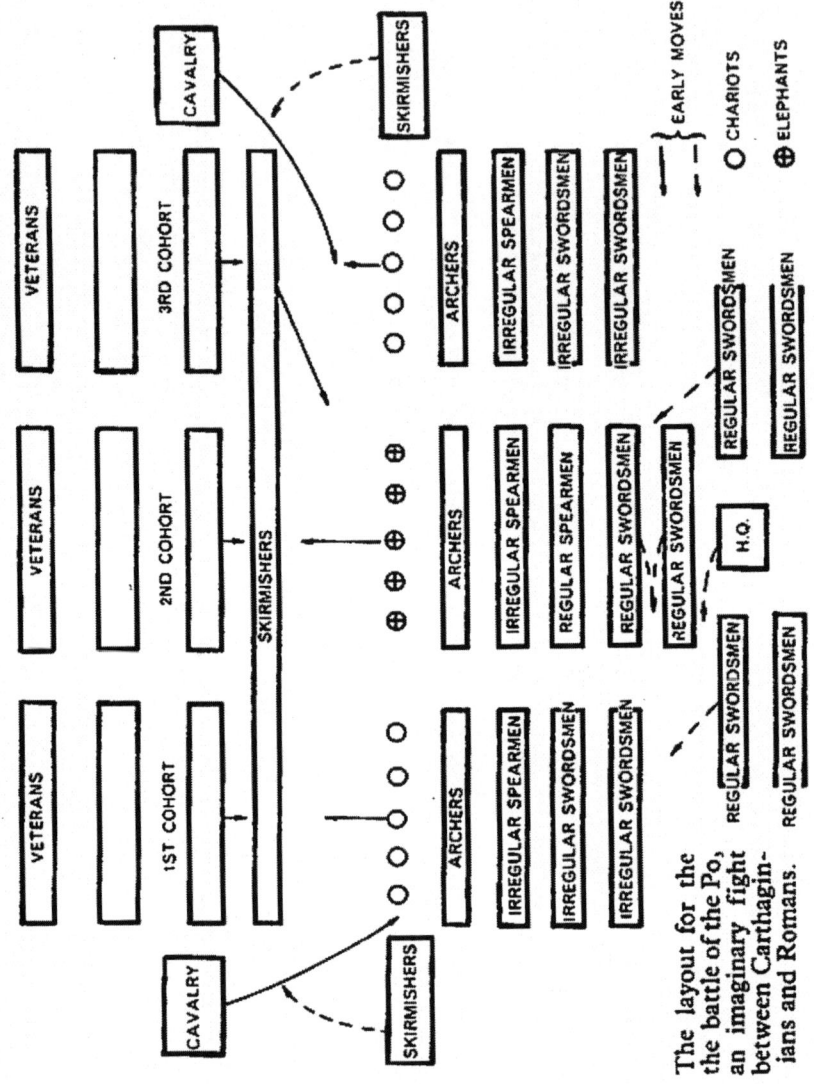

The layout for the the battle of the Po, an imaginary fight between Carthaginians and Romans.

Men bearing shields in mêlées have their casualties reduced by half, unless they are attacked from the rear. Standard bearers are not normally removed as casualties since they serve to identify the various units, but an occasion may arise at the end of a mêlée where they are the only pieces left. In this case they must be surrendered to honour the score of the opponent.

Cavalry count as two points in mêlées, unless wearing heavy plate armour or bearing shields, in which case they count as three points. If cavalry charge into retreating infantry every cavalryman counts as three points regardless of equipment.

If an artillery piece is overrun, the owner may throw a dice. If he scores a six, it is considered put out of action. If he declines this opportunity, his opponent may try for a six. If the piece is not put out of action the winner of the mêlée may remove the piece as and when possible.

Men inside buildings have their casualties halved.

Elephants in mêlées kill all infantry in a line 2 in. directly ahead. If opposed by cavalry, normal mêlée rules apply, the men in the howdahs counting as two points each. If opposed by chariots a six will destroy chariot and crew, otherwise normal mêlée rules apply, the men in the chariots counting as two points each. If cavalry or chariots throw two consecutive sixes the elephant is killed but not the crew.

Chariots kill all infantry in a line 1 in. directly ahead. If opposed by cavalry, normal rules apply.

It will be noted from this that chariots have all the speed and two to one strength of cavalry, plus the advantage that when a crew has been killed the driver may retreat, obtain a fresh crew and re-enter the battle.

Isolation and prisoners

If, when a mêlée takes place, one side has no support troops within one move of the point of impact then it is considered isolated. During the mêlée either side may call for a count. If the isolated men are found to be half the number of their opponents they are taken prisoner.

Prisoners are escorted towards the rear by one sentry to every six men. If prisoners are freed by the death of their sentries they may not move until their commander makes his *next* move. New sentries will probably be supplied before they can get away, but should men not be available for this then an odd situation could arise in which a band of escaped prisoners would be busily dodging about behind the enemy lines in an attempt to reach their own lines without being recaptured.

Morale

If a player's Headquarters is wiped out or if his forces are reduced to less than half he must at once begin to retreat from the board, retiring behind his start line. If his Headquarters are captured he has one more move in which to rescue them. If this fails he must begin to withdraw from the board.

The Battle of the Po

A sample game between Rome and Carthage when Hannibal crossed the Alps. The action takes place on the flat plains between Turin—which was sacked by Hannibal—and Alessandria. The Romans have three cohorts of 60 men, 30 auxiliaries and 18 cavalry, total 210 infantry and 18 cavalry. Hannibal has 11 chariots, five elephants and

200 infantry consisting of about half regulars with shields and half lightly armed irregulars. The Romans have the advantage that all the legionaries bear shields, but the Carthaginians can muster 70 archers (half of them in chariots or on elephants) against the Romans' 20.

Move 1

Rome wins the toss but declines to move! Hannibal sends in the chariots on his left to soften the opposing flank. The infantry there also advance but a band of skirmishers on the extreme left stay back in case of a flank attack by the Roman cavalry.

The two forces face each other before the first move, Romans on the right.

Move 2

The Roman cavalry on the right advances, by-passing the charging chariots which hit the skirmish line. Hannibal orders forward his centre to cover the exposed right of his left wing and the Roman centre also advances. Firing now takes place. Romans: 10 men = 1 dice, scores 4. Target protected by their chariots = 2 men taken. Carthaginians: left wing 10 men in chariots = 1 dice, scores 5. Five skirmishers taken. Centre 25 men = 3 dice. Six = a centurion taken, 5 and 4 (only half of 4 counted as 3rd dice was for 5 men firing), total 7. Targets have shields = 3½, to the nearest unit = 4 men taken. A mêlée is also formed on the left where the chariots have hit the Roman skirmishers.

Carthaginians | *Romans*
6 = 6 men taken (no shields) | 5 = 2½, 3 charioteers taken
5 = ½ taken | 4 = 2 charioteers taken
5 = 2½, 3 men taken | 3 = 1½, 2 charioteers taken

By the third throw there are no charioteers left and the mêlée ends. Roman losses so far are 22, Carthaginians nine men and four chariots.

Move 3

The Roman cavalry on the right wing avoids the enemy skirmishers and swoops round to the rear in a bold attempt to destroy Hannibal himself! The Roman infantry charge to support them and Hannibal halts his left to receive the charge.

In the centre the Romans open their ranks to allow the elephants to pass through, the two rear ranks waiting to receive them with volleys of pilums. Hannibal halts his centre also.

On the Roman left the skirmishers and cavalry charge across to catch the elephants from side and rear, a rash move. Hannibal sends his right wing chariots to stop them, at the same time sending his whole right wing to the attack.

In the rear he cannot bring his reserves up fast enough to save his Headquarters and is forced to pull back the last two ranks of the centre. His reserves close up to cut off the Roman cavalry and support the weakened centre. Firing. Roman: centre only—30 men, 3 dice, score 4, 5, 3 = 12. Target is men on elephants who count as 2 = 6 taken. Carthaginians: left wing 10 men, 1 dice, score 4 = 2 with shields taken. Centre 22 men, 2 dice, score 5,3 = 8. Four with shields taken. Mêlée in centre, elephants against skirmishers.

Carthaginians | *Romans*
3 = 3 taken | 2 = 1 taken from howdah
4 = 4 taken | 4 = 2 taken from howdah

No skirmishers left, mêlée ends. Another mêlée takes place between Roman cavalry and chariots..

Carthaginians | *Romans*
5 = 2½, 3 cavalry taken | 6 = 3 charioteers taken
5 = 2½, 3 cavalry taken | 6 = 3 charioteers taken
4 = 2 cavalry taken | 4 = 2 charioteers taken

Hannibal calls for a count. The surviving Roman cavalry are outnumbered two to one and taken prisoner. The chariots prepare to retire with prisoners and obtain new crews.

End of 3rd move. Roman cavalry (top left) are threatening Hannibal with capture, forcing him to weaken his centre. Roman cavalry on the near flank, attempting to attack the elephants, have been stopped by a chariot attack (right centre).

Move 4

On the Roman right the opposing forces come into contact and a major mêlée begins. The front rank of Romans discharge their pilums, killing four, and take another 16 in the mêlée. The Carthaginians, irregulars without shields, take only nine Romans.

The Roman cavalry, originally aiming at Hannibal himself, swerves to avoid the build-up of reserves and hits the weakened centre instead. Although these are shield-bearing regulars they are caught from behind, the cavalrymen count as three points each, and the Romans take 18 for the loss of only five. At the same time the Roman centre hits the reeling Carthaginians from the front and shatters them completely. If the two ranks of veterans, now dealing with the elephants, could have been there the Carthaginian centre would now have been outnumbered and forced to surrender. In four moves they would have been reduced by a third and the remainder split in half!

Hannibal surrounds the Roman cavalry. On the right flank his archers fire on the advancing Romans, then retreat through the spearmen to mount the chariots waiting in the rear.

In the Roman rear the veterans have killed the occupiers of three howdahs but have been delayed so long by this action that they will never be able to catch up with their front line.

Move 4. Hand-to-hand fighting in the centre and background. The elephants are being dealt with in the rear and the Carthaginian centre is crumbling under attacks from front and rear. In the left foreground the Carthaginian chariots withdraw after annihilating the Roman cavalry there.

Move 5

The Roman cavalry are now finished off", but not before they take another 16 irregulars with them. Hannibal has to commit his personal bodyguard of five cavalry and five archers in an attempt to form a line in the centre. The Roman centre continues the attack, the veterans in the rear now losing four men to stampeding elephants.

All Carthaginian reserves are now committed to hold the centre. A major mêlée is about to start on the right of the picture. Note the skirmishers have outflanked the Roman line (extreme right).

89

The Roman right presses in to continue the mêlée on that flank and inflicts terrible casualties on the lightly armed skirmishers—12 taken for the loss of only six. Hannibal commits his shield-bearing reserves to strengthen the wing. On the Roman left the two wings come into close contact, the Romans being outflanked by skirmishers who remove half of the two front ranks before being wiped out themselves.

Move 6

On Hannibal's left the archers form a last stand whilst the mêlée continues. The Romans lose six men but score 6,6,6,4. The Carthaginians lose three officers in three throws and are suddenly leaderless. They turn to run in confusion, breaking up the archers' line.

In the centre the Roman veterans have at last finished off the elephants. The mêlée continues near Hannibal, reserve ranks from the Roman left moving up to reinforce the centre. But they are too late. The Romans lose eight, Carthaginians nine but Hannibal's mounted bodyguard save the day by outnumbering the surviving Romans two to one. The Romans are taken prisoner, leaving a big hole in the centre.

On the Roman left the Carthaginians save themselves by mounting their archers in the chariots, thus doubling their value. After the mêlée the Romans call for a count—Romans 31, Carthaginians 22. No decision.

Move 6. On the right Roman reserves try to move across to help their centre but are too late. Carthaginian archers in the foreground are retiring to mount the waiting chariots.

Move 7

The victorious Roman right sends one rank to finish off the retreating Carthaginians while the rest turn towards the centre to rescue their comrades taken prisoner. Hannibal leads three chariots against them in an attempt to reach his left and rally them. The Romans lose four, but four out of eight charioteers are killed and Hannibal is threatened with capture. He has failed in his attempt to supply his left with an officer.

In the centre a thin line of Carthaginians holds on grimly as the Romans move in for the kill. The Roman left fails to make headway although they manage to empty two out of three chariots there.

Move 8

Hannibal now tries to make a last stand in the centre but, attacked front and left, he loses six men to the Romans' two. However, one of the men lost by the Romans was their only centurion on the right and they are forced to stop. Hannibal, with over half his surviving men in full retreat, seizes the opportunity to order retreat, taking his prisoners with him. The Romans, with no cavalry left to pursue, have to let him get away.

Move 7 The Carthaginians have broken (cop left) and are in retreat with Hannibal attempting to reach them. Left of centre are survivors of the Roman attack on the centre being led away as prisoners.

The final scene as the defeated Carthaginians run from the field. Left foreground the Roman prisoners are ushered into captivity.

If the scoring system, described in Chapter 9, had been used the result would have been as follows: Romans 50 points for winning, points for men, chariots, etc., = 193½ . Carthaginians = 118.

Chapter 7 The Rules for the Horse and Musket Era

Movement Rules

All the rules for this era follow closely on the basic lines of those in the preceding chapter, but there is one vital change in the movement rules. In the musket era reloading was a lengthy business and because of this no man or artillery piece may move *and* fire. This ruling can cause confusion on a busy board, for it is not always possible to remember every single man's actions. The system of written orders erases such errors and is of great help in this era. Scale of moves:

    Infantry, horse-drawn heavy artillery and wagons, 6 in.
    Horse artillery, cavalry and staff officers, 12 in.
    Guns moved by hand, 3 in.
    All pieces moving on roads have their move increased by a third.

    Artillery take one move to ascend or descend a hill, half a move to limber or unlimber and may only cross rivers by bridges or fords. If crews are killed they may be replaced by other pieces.

    Cavalry and infantry may cross rivers anywhere but their move is reduced by 50 per cent unless using a bridge or ford. They may pass over walls and fences under 1 in. in height. Infantry may climb higher walls but their move is reduced by half.

    Cavalry and infantry must be led by an officer when advancing. If infantry lose all officers whilst advancing they must be turned to face the rear and retreat on the next move, continuing to retreat until another officer is sent to lead them. Once cavalry have begun a charge they cannot be halted by loss of officers, but if they are not charging when they lose their officers they must turn and retreat on the next move, continuing to retreat until another officer is sent to lead them. If retreating infantry are forced into a river, except at a ford, they lose a third of their number in crossing.

Firing Rules

Cavalry and infantry armed with muskets may fire up to a range of 12 in. Only the front ranks may fire unless two ranks have been staggered or the front rank is kneeling down.

    For each ten men throw one dice, the score indicating the number of casualties. Fractions of ten above 5 count at half score, those below 5 are disregarded.

    Every six that is scored removes an officer. If two consecutive sixes arc thrown a staff officer may be removed if in range: if three consecutive sixes are thrown the commanding general may be removed if in range.

    Men under cover of buildings, walls, hedges, etc., have the casualties halved. Cavalrymen and gunners count as two points each.

Produced by Airfix the fort makes a useful outpost for most periods.

The Airfix wagon train set, ideal for supply wagons and Boers with their families in commando

Artillery ranges:
Horse Artillery, 24 in.
Heavy artillery, 36 in.
Grape-shot instead of round shot or shell may be used at a range of 6 in. or less.

An extra limber made from the front axle assembly of an Airfix Wagon Train set, wheels from a spare gun, and box built up with balsa. Towing hook is wire.

Horse artillery may only fire on the front ranks of the enemy, unless it has been sited on hills. Heavy artillery may fire on any troops in range. Horse artillery must also have a clear view of their target and may not fire through their own formations. If the view is masked they may not fire. Before any gun is fired the player must state his target area.

Two dice are thrown for each gun to register a hit or a miss; 7-12 hit, 1-6 miss. If a hit is scored each gun takes four casualties if it has a full crew of four, three for a crew of three, two for a crew of two and one for a crew of one.

If a six is thrown an officer may be removed, together with other pieces to make up the score on the other dice. If a double six is thrown a staff officer, wagon, gun or limber may be removed. The crews are not killed.

All firing at 6 in. and below is considered a hit but the two dice are still thrown to see if any officers are to be removed. The normal scores for guns, in proportion to their crews, are doubled because grape-shot is used at this short range.

Mêlée Rules

Artillery and infantry on the nearby flanks may not fire into a mêlée. Pieces engaged in a mêlée are all those within a 6 in. radius of the point of impact.

Each player throws a dice 4 times and removes the number of men indicated by the dice. A 6 takes an officer, two consecutive sixes a staff officer if available.

If one side is totally removed before or by the end of the four throws then he has naturally lost. If any officers are left they must fall back on the nearest friendly troops in range. If unable to do this they are taken prisoner.

Ensigns or colour sergeants are not normally removed as casualties but must be surrendered if necessary to honour a score.

Cavalrymen count as two points, three if charging into the rear of retreating infantry.

If a gun is overrun by infantry and not spiked by a throw of six the winner of the mêlée may take the gun away. The limber and crew of horse artillery may gallop clear. If the gun is overrun by cavalry a normal mêlée ensues, with both gunners and cavalry counting as two points each.

The rules for Isolation, Prisoners and Morale are the same as those for Ancient Warfare.

The Sample Game of the Battle of Centreville

A sample game set in the American Civil War. Each side has 3 regiments of infantry—81 men—with 3 guns and a squadron of cavalry—12 men. The Confederates win the toss and make the surprising decision to fight from the open side of the board. By coincidence both players decide to attack on their left flanks, leaving only light forces to hold their right.

Move 1

On the Confederate (CSA) left the 8th Georgia advance towards Twin Buttes, their supporting gun advancing with them. To their right one company of Texans crosses the River Road in support. These initial moves are part of the plan to capture Stone bridge.

On the Federal (USA) left the first companies of the 8th Massachusetts and 107th Ohio cross the Centreville Road. This is the beginning of the USA attack along the turnpike to West bridge.

No firing may take place.

Move 2

One company of Georgians occupies the north side of Twin Buttes and the gun is taken up the hill. The other two companies pass Stone house, using it for cover as much as possible.

Two more companies of the Texans are now committed, the CSA general deciding to ignore the moves against his right flank.

The USA general also decides he can hold his right whilst continuing his advance on the left and sends forward the regiment of Zouaves and the remainder of 8th Mass. Out of 9 companies he has now committed 7 to the attack along the turnpike.

Firing. CSA: On the left all troops have moved—no firing. Centre gun fires, scores a double six but there is no gun, limber or staff officer in range. Four men, under cover = 2 taken. The gun on the right fails to score over 6 and misses. Ten men, 1 dice, score 2=1 man taken. USA: left-hand gun fires on Bald Hill. Hit, 2 taken. Centre gun fires on advancing Texans. Hit = 4 men taken. Ten men on Signal Peak fire, 1 dice, score 3 = 3 taken. The Texan officer has to move back as he is now some 3 in. in front of his surviving men. The right-hand gun misses.

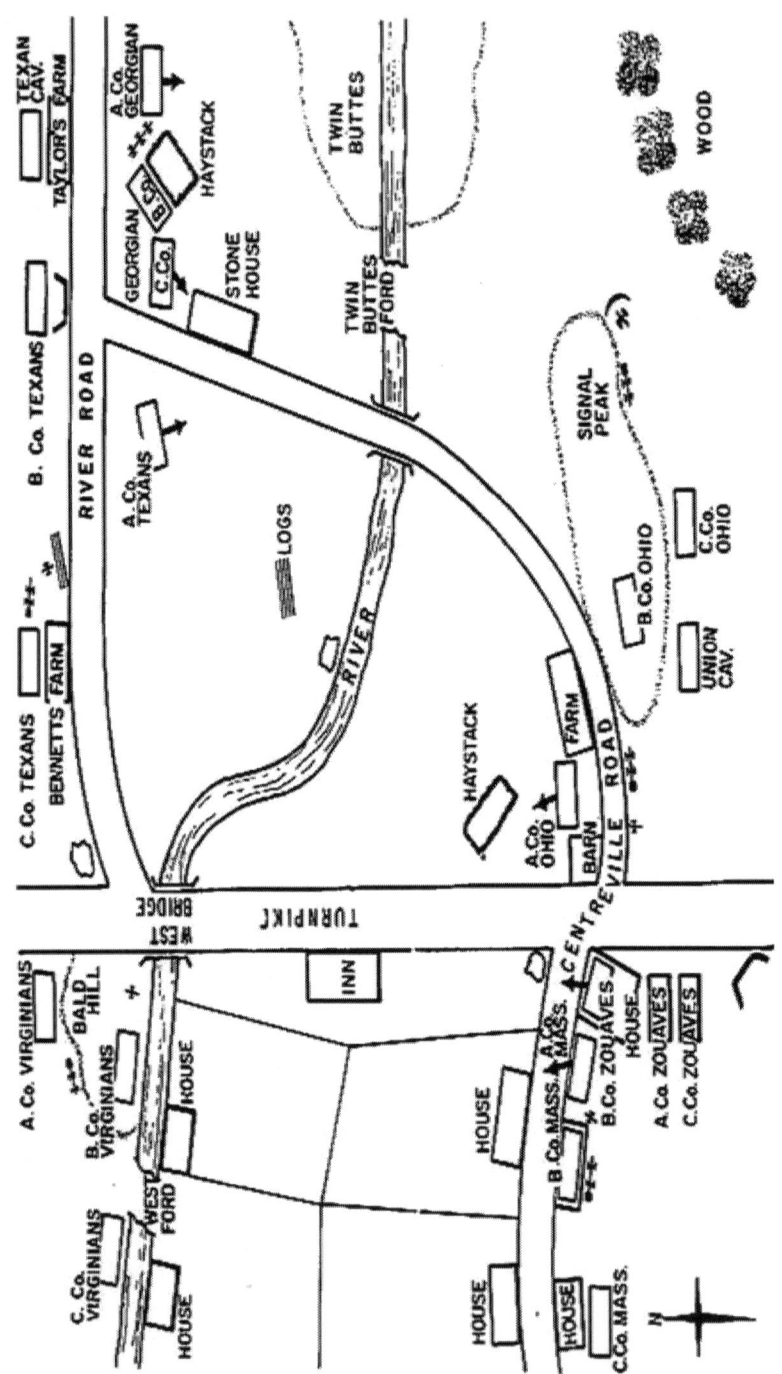

The Battle for Centreville at the end of the first move. Note the extensive use of cover by both sides

Move 3

Some Georgians cross to the south side of Twin Buttes whilst others with the Texans cross Stone bridge. The CSA cavalry leaves Taylor's farm and, using the roads, advances swiftly in support.

Seeing this the USA commander makes a rash move and commits "his cavalry, intended to back up his own attack on West bridge, in a counter-attack at Stone bridge. However, he continues his infantry attack down the turnpike. CSA take 6 men, USA take 11 men and an officer, half of them from the attack on Stone bridge.

Move 4. First units of Federal troops reach West Bridge. In the background can be see the mass of rebel troops using the road over Stone Bridge to advance swiftly on Signal Peak.

Move 4

Ignoring the threat at Bald Hill the CSA press home their attack across Stone bridge. The USA attacks West bridge to cut the rebel forces in two. USA cavalry moves in to attack the CSA cavalry. USA take 10 men, 8 from the attack over Stone bridge, but the CSA, using grapeshot, pound the attack on West bridge from their strongpoint on Bald Hill and take 14 men. The officer leading the attack has to be moved back and the heavy losses cause the advance to be delayed one move while reinforcements are brought up.

Move 5

The Texan cavalry suddenly dart round the near end of Signal Peak to attack the gun there, exposing the advancing USA cavalry to a fire from over 20 men and 2 guns. In the firing that follows the USA cavalry is reduced to half strength. However, the USA attack on West bridge is pushed home and a mêlée joined, the over-confident CSA general committing his Headquarters in an attempt to gain a victory on this flank too. In the mêlée USA lose 9 to the CSA's 6 in the first three throws, then call for a count. The CSA are outnumbered 17 to 8 and the entire rebel Headquarters is captured.

Move 5. Survivors of the leading Confederate company (centre) attack Signal Peak. Their cavalry, having drawn the Union cavalry out of cover, now dives, round the near end of Signal Peak, forcing the gun there to abandon its emplacement. Federal infantry form a line to try to stop them.

Move 5. The fight for West Bridge. A depleted company of Virginians hurry to assist, abandoning West ford which they have been guarding. Extreme left is the HQ that is about to be captured in the mêlée.

Move 6

The CSA must rescue their general or concede defeat and all available troops are moved in by both sides for a fresh mêlée at West bridge. USA score 2, 4, 1, 3: CSA score 6, 4, 2, 3 but despite this fail to gain a decision and their Headquarters are moved away as prisoners.

At the other end of the board the rebel cavalry are having a field day mopping up fragments of cavalry and infantry. They take 5 prisoners and the Federals only just save their gun there, but in the following move CSA must begin to withdraw from the board.

Moves 7, 8 and 9 are taken up in a fighting retreat by CSA who now lose heavily to the USA guns, although the Federals have no cavalry left to turn the defeat into a rout.

Using the scoring system mentioned in the previous chapter the Federals would have had 179 points to the rebels 150. Since the USA had 50 points for winning it can be seen that even at the end of the game the CSA forces were superior to those of the Federals, and the result could have been far different if only the CSA player had not used his Headquarters as fighting men!

Move 6. Union troops fall back from West bridge with their important prisoners but exert pressure on West ford, now unguarded. The rebels begin to retreat

Chapter 8 The Rules for Modern Warfare (2nd World War)

Movement Rules

Fighting during the Second World War was on a much wider front, with a huge array of supporting land, sea and air weapons, than any war in history. Because of this movement rules need to be reconsidered extensively.

Attempting to reconstruct the huge battles on a small game board is impossible and the best way to overcome the sheer size of modern campaigns is to use a map of the area to manoeuvre your armies, moving to a game board only for small, local rights, and deducting the casualties for each of these battles from the armies engaged in the campaign as a whole.

By reducing movement scales to a minimum it is possible to have a fair amount of movement on a small board. To achieve this I suggest discarding the inch as a basic measurement, switching to the centimetre instead. If one centimetre (cm) represents i m.p.h. then an infantryman would move— on average—5 cm or 2 in. If this seems a tiny move remember that in this era most infantry moves can be made by the use of vehicles.

Similarly a tank moving across country could move at 15 m.p.h., or 15 cm, about 6 in., and a scout car moving along a road at 40 m.p.h. would cover 40 cm or approximately 16 in. Charles Grant, in a series of articles on battle gaming for the *Meccano Magazine,* has suggested using the inch measurement on the same principle. This is merely a matter of personal choice, influenced by the size of your board.

Obviously different types of tanks or other vehicles would move at varying speeds, but for simplicity an average has been taken. The comparison between speeds on metalled roads and across country has been maintained by the bonus system for roads, though this has been increased from a third to half for tracked vehicles and infantry, and by 100 per cent for wheeled vehicles. The following scale should clarify these points.

The British 25-pounder, used throughout the Second World War, remained in service until 1968.

The German 88 mm tankbuster with its powerful tractor. Both pieces, by Airfix, are great assets in modern battle gaming[5].

---

[5] Modern meant World War II to the early wargamers.

An egg box gun emplacement. The guns may be elevated to 45 degrees. Flock could be used to give a better camouflage effect

Pill boxes made from the bottom half of the same egg box.

Movement Scale:

Tracked Vehicles—50 per cent increase on roads.
  S.P. guns, halftracks: across country 10 cm, 4 in.
  Tanks: across country 15 cm. 6 in.

Wheeled Vehicles—100 per cent increase on roads.
  Scout cars, armoured cars, jeeps and staff cars: across country 20 cm, 8 in.
  All other wheeled transport: across country 15 cm, 6 in.

Infantry: across country 5 cm, 2 in.: on roads 7 cm, approx. 3 in.

These scales are not meant to infer that each move takes one hour to complete, since the amount of firing to take place per move would then be colossal in comparison!

All vehicles and guns may only cross rivers by bridges, fords or where engineers are erecting pontoon bridges or manning boats.

Artillery take one move to ascend or descend a hill, half a move to limber or unlimber

Infantry may cross rivers anywhere but have their move reduced by half unless using a ford or bridge.

The rules concerning officers leading all advances does not apply in this type of warfare.

All pieces may move *and* fire except machine guns, mortars and artillery. (S.P. guns do not come under this restriction.)

Firing Rules

Because of the vast variety of weapons involved two scales are necessary, for not only do we have to consider a weapon's killing power but also its effective range. The ranges have been determined in relation to moves rather than scaling down real distances. All tanks and artillery fire *twice* in each move.

Range Scale:

Pistol, sub machine gun, grenade, flame thrower, 5 cm, 2 in.
Rifles, machine guns, 20 cm, 8 in.
Anti tank and S.P. guns, armoured cars, mortars, light and medium tanks 40 cm, 16 in.
Heavy tanks and Artillery, 60 cm, 24 in.

It has been calculated that in the Second World War it took a thousand bullets to kill a man. Certainly it cannot be assumed that, even at close ranges, hits were certain—or had any effect. Therefore, all firing is subjected to a hit or miss rule.

Two dice are thrown to indicate hit or miss and casualties are removed at the corresponding rates shown below. All men under cover have casualties reduced by half, odd halves counting as one.

Effect Scale.	Hit	*Casualties*
Pistol, rifle.	6 or over	1 man
Sub machine gun.	6 or over	1 men
Machine gun, grenade, flame thrower.	6 or over	3 men

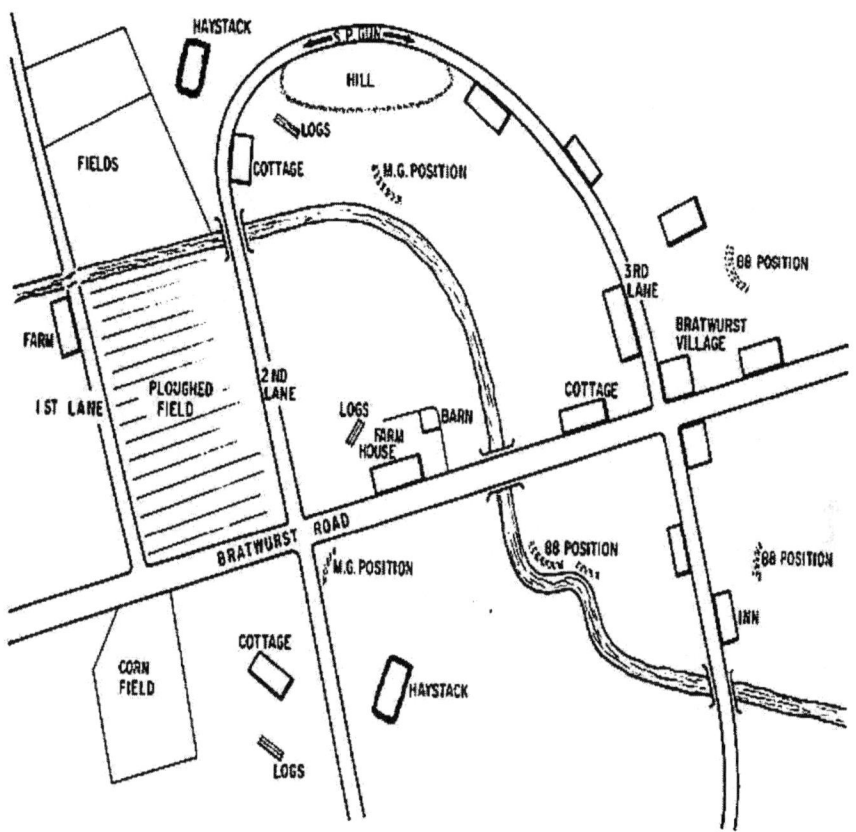

The layout for the Bratwurst village battle. Note how big areas have been broken up with buildings or oddments.

Armoured car, mortar. 6 or over all within a 5 cm radius S.P. guns, light and
medium tanks.   6 or over   all within 10 cm radius
Heavy artillery and
tanks.   6 or over   all within a 15 cm radius
Anti-tank guns,
bazookas.   11 or 12 destroys any tank.

(If playing a series of games to form a campaign 9, 10 or 11 could damage a tank, 12 destroy it. This way damaged tanks could be towed away by either side and repaired, to enter another battle later in the series.)

Officers who are included in the radius of a shell burst are taken, but where individuals are removed, the first three items on the scale, then an officer may only be removed if the dice show a double.

Any gun that scores a double six whilst aiming at an opposing gun takes that piece from the board. Any double will take any 'soft-skinned' vehicle.

Any tank that scores a double six whilst aiming at an opposing tank takes that piece from the board. Any double takes any 'soft-skinned' vehicle.

Any tank or artillery piece firing on enemy Headquarters in the open may remove it from the board if they score a double six. It is vital, therefore, to see that Headquarters are always under cover, thus qualifying for the halved rate of casualties and preventing them being wiped out by a solitary shell.

Mêlée Rules

These will rarely take place, since most infantry in modern warfare prefer to remain under cover! Should they occur, the normal rules apply.

The rules for Isolation, Prisoners and Morale are the same as those for the two previous eras, with the addition that any side without officers, apart from the Headquarters staff, must retreat from the board.

The Attack on Bratwurst Village

A sample game in Europe early in 1945. This differs from the previous sample games in that the Germans are placed in a strong defensive position in depth whilst the British are only making a reconnaissance in strength. The players toss for choice of sides.

Both players have a company of infantry, approximately 100 men each, but the Germans have 3 Tiger tanks, three 88 mm a/t guns, 3 armoured cars, an S.P., 3 half-track personnel carriers, 3 Pak a/t guns and 6 panzerfausts against the British 4 Churchills, 3 bren gun carriers, three 6-pounders, two 25-pounders and 3 half-track personnel carriers with machine guns. Owing to the nature of the game, with the British moving on to the edge of the board from the left, firing is to take place from the end of the first move.

Move 1

The British commander has no idea where the a/t guns and machine guns are hidden, and cannot see many of the infantry or even two of the tanks! Therefore he sends a platoon of infantry in to draw fire and clear any snipers from the cover by the first lane. The platoon enters the board on both sides of the river. The Germans open fire.

Two sub-machine guns throw 5, 7. One hit = 2 men taken.
Grenade throws 9. Hit = 3 men but only 1 in range.
Armoured car throws 8 and 5. One hit = 2 men in radius of 5 cm.
British infantry reply: 7 rifles score 4 hits = 4 under cover, 2 taken.

Grenade scores a hit = 3 men under cover = *1$*. Two men should be taken but only 1 is in range.

Move 1. British infantry move on to the board, searching for snipers

Move 2

The British infantry reach cover; the section on the left begins to cross open fields. A Churchill tank enters on the right flank.

The Germans fire: 5 rifles, 3 hits (including a double 6 but no officer available) = 3 men, under cover = 1½ . Two taken.

Three armoured cars score 3 hits but the infantry are very scattered and only 2 men are within each shell burst. Being under cover only one man is taken for each hit. The S.P. opens fire on approaching infantry and scores a hit, 2 men in 10 cm radius; both taken.

The British reply: 7 rifles, 4 hits = 4, under cover, 2 taken.

Churchill machine guns score a hit = 3, under cover, 2 taken.

The tank also fires its gun twice but misses.

Move 3

The two 25-pounders arrive and unlimber under cover. Company H.Q. arrives too and a second tank is brought up on the left together with a half-track full of infantry. The other two sections of number 2 platoon advance, the centre one on foot and the right flank one in a half-track. German firing, although scoring many hits, takes only 5 men as the British are now widely deployed. However, the S.P. scores a hit with a double six and takes 3 men in a 10 cm radius, including the first platoon officer and wireless operator. The British reply and take 4 men, the Churchill missing again!

Move 3. The build up of British forces prior to the attack across the fields and against the crossroads.

Move 4

The British infantry begin their advance across the open, supported by 2 tanks and two 25-pounders. Three bren gun carriers are suddenly brought forward on the right and advance to outflank the armoured car that the Churchill has now missed four times. The armoured car pulls out hurriedly and retreats up the main road. The Germans take six of the advancing infantry, 5 with rifle fire, whilst the British take 7.

Move 5

The British advance continues and 2 more tanks arrive with the other 2 half-tracks full of infantry and towing two 6-pounders. A German panzerfaust team opens fire but misses. The German first platoon leader, with his H.Q. in the farmhouse on the centre of the Bratwurst road, leads a small counter-attack and in the resulting exchange of shots the British lose 5 to the Germans' 9. The Churchills destroy 2 panzerfaust teams.

Move 4. The advance begins: the first wave of infantry cross the fields, the second wave waiting under cover.

Move 6

The British half-tracks arrive at the crossroads and begin to unload the infantry. One 25-pounder limbers up, ready to move up in close support. The defeated and outnumbered German first platoon withdraws across the river, leaving the British apparently triumphant. However, the German 88s and Tigers are about to enter the action. The British take 4 men and a tank destroys another panzerfaust team, losing 5 men in return. Two panzerfausts fire on the leading Churchill, score a hit and succeed in knocking it out.

Move 7

The British tanks halt whilst their infantry advance to secure the farmhouse in the centre. Two 6-pounders go into action against the Tiger hiding behind the haystack on the right. Other artillery begins to close up. The German Tiger holds on stubbornly and 2 armoured cars, accompanied by a half-track full of infantry, make the first move towards assisting it. German firing takes 9 men, a panzerfaust scores a double six to take one of the 6-pounders and a Tiger scores a double one to destroy the leading half-track. The British take only 4 men. This is the turning point of the game.

Move 7. The choked road to the British rear that cramped their manoeuvering. By the crossroads a half track and 6-pounder have been destroyed

Move 8

The British 25-pounders go into action again, the advance continues left and centre on the bridge, but the right is held up by the Tiger behind the haystack. The 2 German armoured cars and half-track cross the bridge by the Inn and move up to reinforce the Tiger. Firing: each side takes 7 men.

Move 9

Two Churchills and supporting infantry attack the hill on the left whilst the infantry in the centre cross the river. The remaining 6-pounder at the crossroads is manhandled into position in an attempt to clear the Tiger on the right but it is already too late. The 2 German armoured cars with their infantry arrive and go into action, the British infantry attacking the bridge suddenly coming under heavy enfilading fire on their exposed right flank. The Germans kill 14 infantry and a Tiger on the German right scores 11 to destroy a Churchill. The British take 6 men and a panzerfaust team.

Move 10

As the British advance falters the Germans launch their counter-attack. It is perfect timing. Heavy armour races down the main road, backed by armoured cars and half-tracks full of infantry, as the German commander commits all his forces except the 88s in the rear. The British have only a 6-pounder a/t gun in the front line: they have lost 2 out of 4 tanks and their only other a/t gun is too far away to be of any use. (It cannot cross the fields which have no suitable exits and must go all the way round by road from the opposite flank.)

The Germans take 11 British infantry, who are caught in mid stream. A Pak gun scores 11 to destroy the other Churchill on the left flank and the Tiger advancing down the main road scores a double six to destroy the last British tank. The 2 armoured cars on the flank fire on a bren gun carrier full of infantry and score double five—carrier destroyed—and 9 = hit. Three men in the radius are taken. The British take 6 men and a 25-pounder scores a double six to destroy the first 88 gun position.

Move 11

The British force is reduced to a shambles of wrecked vehicles. The remaining 2 half-tracks load up with infantry and beat a hasty retreat, covered by the 6-pounder and two 25-pounders. The German armour races ahead, trying to cut off the British. On the German left, where the 6-pounder is holding out, the 2 armoured cars take a chance and advance across the open on the gun. British firing is haphazard and the Germans suffer no casualties. They take 9 men and a Tiger scores a .direct hit on a half-track, killing 7 men in the back—all in the 15 cm radius!

Move 12

The British force races for their start line with the German armour in hot pursuit. The Germans take another 8 men without loss to themselves.

On the next move the game ends. Using the scoring system the result would have been: Germans 302, British 141. Out of approximately 100 men the British managed to save only 20, 24 men being lost in the retreat alone.

The Germans advance unopposed, except for a grenade thrower and two men with a machine-gun on the destroyed Churchill in the foreground.

Detailed models by Minitanks, from the left: jeep with machine gun, jeep with anti-tank gun, Dodge command car with canopy up or down. In front are two motor-cyclists.

Chapter 9 Variations of the Game

A scoring system

In the previous chapters reference has been made to a system of scoring. Experience has shown that despite rules to cover morale, prisoners, etc., many generals insist on playing battle games that are nothing more than blood baths, using their armies to fight grimly on to the very last man. The points system is intended to stop this.

The winner of a game would receive 50 points: other points are awarded as follows:

1 point for every surviving foot soldier, including officers.
2 points for every surviving mounted soldier, including officers.
½ point for every prisoner, excluding officers.
½ point for every man held prisoner by the enemy, including officers.
5 points for every foot officer held prisoner. 10 points for every mounted officer held prisoner.
5 points for every gun limber.
5 points for every machine gun.
10 points for every field gun, a/t gun, armoured car, bren gun carrier.
15 points for every tank, S.P. or heavy artillery piece.
5 points for every damaged enemy tank captured.
10 points for every chariot.
10 points for every elephant.

The score is totalled at the end of a game, that is when one side has admitted defeat and withdrawn behind their start line

This method encourages realism, since when a staff officer worth 10 points, or a tank worth 15, is threatened with capture most players will retreat to fight another day. Also when a player feels he has lost a game he will surrender the field by a skilful retreat rather than staying to fight to the last man. A commander should be able to retire in good order, taking as many of his opponent's pieces as possible, yet preserving his own. During such a retreat a player may decide to surrender some men who are too deeply committed to be withdrawn, thus slowing his opponent's advance by taking men for escort duty!

By this method a rubber of games could be played, enabling whole campaigns to be fought over a period of time. This way a player could lose two out of three battles yet still win the campaign—a victory is no victory if all your men are dead.

A game can, of course, be fought to the finish if players prefer, but this is neither realistic nor so skilful and players who choose this method will discover it is not so exciting either.

A solo game

Battle gaming is such an absorbing hobby that there is no need for any player to become bored with it—even if he always has to play against himself. In some ways a solo game has advantages—the main one being that there is no time limit and he can return to the game again and again over a period of weeks if necessary whereas most dual games are restricted to an evening or a Sunday afternoon.

It is possible to play against yourself with the rules already set down here but I must confess that when I have done this there has always been a slight prejudice to one side—and you always know what the 'other fellow' is planning to do next. The best answer is to try to be impartial and make your moves as the game develops instead of planning ahead, making your 'favourite' army weaker than the other. This does give a reasonable solo game.

Another method is to reduce battle gaming into a game of chance, but retaining some of the skill. Make a pack of 52 blank cards from paper or cardboard and mark them in the following way:

Dover Patrol, a lively battle game with complications caused mainly by a seaplane that 'jumps' unexpectedly over the harbour wall to occupy your base.

10 cards. Move 1 company of infantry, 1 squadron of cavalry or tanks or HQ.
8 cards. Move 2 companies of infantry, or 1 gun or tank.
4 cards. Move 1 regiment or 2 guns.
2 cards. Move 2 regiments or 3 guns.
1 card. Move 1 brigade.*
2 cards. Take 1 staff officer.*

3 cards. Take 1 foot officer.
4 cards. Take 1 gun, limber or tank.
2 cards. Take 1 company of infantry or 4 cavalry.*
4 cards. Take 6 infantry or 2 cavalry.
10 cards. Take 4 infantry or 1 cavalry.
2 cards. Take 2 men for every gun in action.*

Mêlées would be ruled by the throw of dice as usual and rules for prisoners, isolation, morale and scoring would all be the same. Cards marked *, of which there are 7, may not be held in the player's hand: they must be used at once or forfeited. All other cards may be held back in the player's hand but no more than three cards may be held at any one time. Movement and Firing cards may be used together, that is one of each, but two Movement or two Firing cards may not. Any card may be used to move, or take, a number of pieces less than that shown on it.

Manufactured games

Waddingtons make many battle games but they are mostly naval; other games are available from America direct or via *Wargamer's Newsletter*. The ones described below are manufactured by Gibsons of London and cover land, sea, air and combined operations. All the games mentioned are played between two players, each player having pieces with different values and purposes, over a marked board.

The rules of Tri-tactics may strike a newcomer as complicated but they are soon picked up. Two cards supplied with the rules contain charts showing what takes what and are of considerable help for the first few games.

Aviation, the air battle game by Gibson

L'Attaque. This is the army game. The board is 12 squares wide, three of which are lakes and cannot be crossed. Each player has in addition four mines and the combinations of these result in too much emphasis on defence and not enough on the much more costly attack! However, there are sappers to deal with the mines and the game is enlivened by the scouts, of which there are eight per side, who can dash from one end of the board to the other and cause considerable inconvenience!

Dover Patrol. This naval game is probably the oldest game of its kind. As the name implies it was first marketed soon after the First World War and I myself have been playing it for the last 20 years. The variety of pieces and their different uses, and the endless combinations in which they may be used, make this a game of which you can never tire.

Aviation. This is the air game which I have never played personally but I have seen the game and it appears to be just as good as the others.

The fourth game, and in my opinion the best, is *Tri-Tactics*. This is a vast combination of land, sea and air forces totalling 56 pieces per player, played on a board of 144 squares, 56 of which are~water and the remainder land.

The pieces include infantry in various strengths, heavy artillery, field artillery, ack ack, reconnaissance aircraft, bombers, fighters, seaplanes, destroyers, cruisers, battleships and a submarine. The aircraft may travel anywhere but armies and navies are supposed to stay in their natural elements. I say supposed to because the pieces are stood upright on metal stands so that the opponent cannot tell their value and therefore a player can move army pieces across the sea or vice versa. If caught doing this he loses the pieces.

A good game, played carefully and craftily, can last from one to two hours and is quite exhausting. It is excellent training for the bigger board and more numerous pieces of battle gaming with models, since a player must have the right pieces in the right place at the right time. If he allows a vital piece to lag too far behind an advance—or worse still lose it—it may cost him the game.

The game is rarely won by the player who ploughs on regardless, taking as many pieces as he can: success is far more likely to go to the player who uses a pincer movement or tries to cut his opponent's forces in half, both of which manoeuvres need considerable skill as much of the attack is launched across the sea.

I have been playing the game for the last seven years, usually two games a week, and cannot remember two games ever developing in exactly the same way.

A new Battle Game introduced by Triang
Photo taken at the Conference of Wargamers in 2009 by Bob Cordery

Chapter 10 Some Ideas for Advanced Players

No doubt while reading the chapters on rules the reader has said to himself—what about minefields, trenches, barbed wire ? The rules are the basis on which to work and have been stripped down to their simplest form: for players who wish to go further, to obtain more realism, here are a few ideas.

Some of the ideas already mentioned, such as written orders, simultaneous moves and beginning a game by approach roads instead of placing all the pieces on the board at the beginning, are improvements that have been made to the older methods of battle gaming and such improvements are constantly cropping up.; The two most popular battle gaming magazines in Britain, *Miniature Warfare* and *Wargamer's Newsletter,* both publish regular articles on new ideas. It is worth contributing to one or both of them in order to keep up with all these ideas.

Campaigns

One idea mentioned earlier, a rubber of games, is worth considering further. An example would be a campaign of perhaps three battles to be fought over a period of time. Both players could start with the same number of troops and the terrain would be altered for each battle. It would be up to each player to decide how many men he would hold in reserve for the next battle. Casualties would not be able to take part in any future batde but vehicles, such as the damaged tanks mentioned earlier, could reappear.

By this method a player, using his pieces with care and preserving life where possible, could lose two out of three battles yet still win the campaign on points. As in real life there would in publication for over nine years. The editor, Donald Featherstone, is the author of many books on battle gaming be no success in winning two out of three battles if your forces were reduced to almost zero whilst your 'defeated' opponent still had considerable forces in the field. Of course, such campaigns need not be restricted to imaginary battles—in fact the reconstruction of real campaigns often provides much more enjoyment.

Trains and boats

Trains add enormously to the swift movement of troops, and to an army's firepower. A train with two wagons full of troops, or carrying guns, moving at perhaps 2 ft a move, would be a great asset. Time would have to be allowed for entraining and detraining, say half a move for each. Trains could also be used as mobile ack ack positions, or adapted as armoured trains such as were used in the Boer War and on the Russian front in the Second World War.

Boats can also be introduced to the board, either in the form of landing craft on a beachhead at one end of the board, or small craft on a river or lake. They could cover 6 in. per move and men could take half a move to embark or disembark. One model train layout I've heard of had a large lake in the centre that was hinged so that it could be dropped down to allow the owner to pop up in the centre of his board!

The railway line as used for the battle of Murfreesboro reconstruction. The small piers in the river are by Playcraft

Railways add speed and excitement to a game. Here points are being heavily defended for if captured the spur line would lead the enemy straight to the rear.

Two 25-pounders and a 6-pounder mounted on railway wagons to make a powerful, fast-moving strike force

A platoon of infantry being rushed across the board to reinforce the opposite flank.

Airfix landing craft in action. Establishing beach heads on one end of the board provides a challenging game.

Obstacles

Troops would naturally erect earthworks if they were holding a position for any length of time. This can be introduced to the game by declaring the intention to erect an earthwork, then maintaining a body of men on that position for two moves. A slit trench would take only one move. At the end of these moves the player would put an entrenchment in position.

Mines can be used but being 'invisible' assets cannot be actually placed on the board. They could, however, be marked on a plan by the player, who would then present the plan in evidence whenever his opponent blew himself up! Sappers would need to remain in position two moves to lay an area of mines or remove them. Another complication to this is whether your mines are anti tank or anti personnel. The latter could kill all men in a 7 cm or 3 in. radius, the former need to throw perhaps a five or six with a dice to destroy a tank, otherwise the tank would be merely damaged. Other types of vehicles would also be destroyed by the anti-tank mine.

A boat made from balsa wood and cardboard being used to transport troops. Where a river cuts a board in half the possession of boats or rubber dinghies is a great asset.

The great possibilities created by using Bellona terrain units are shown here. The Fortified Beach Position and Wharf set have been combined to form an objective, which has been fortified with "dragon's teeth", pill boxes and the like, providing an "instant" terrain worth fighting over.

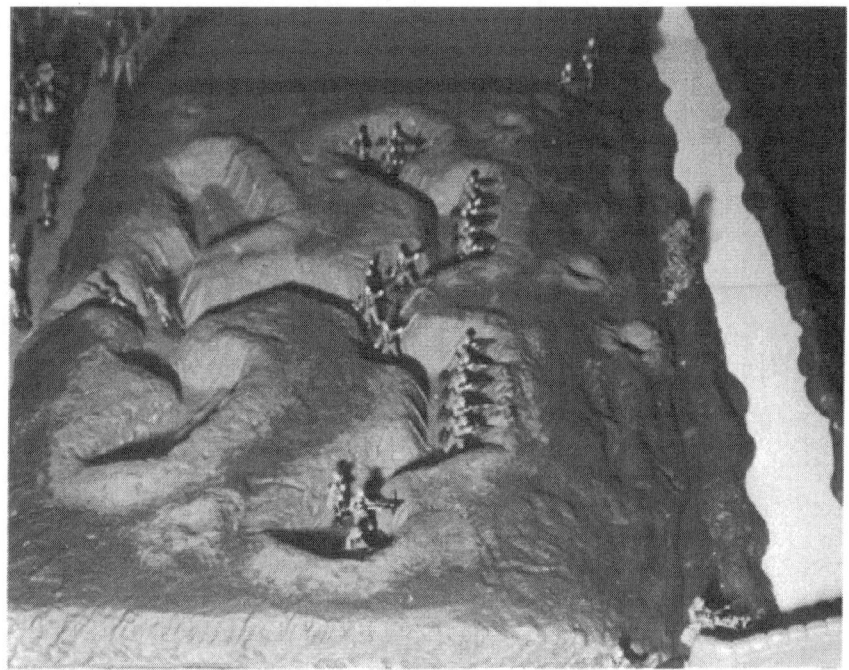

Bellona's 1914-18 trench system which will suit most eras. Additional realism can be gained by sticking on some lichen.

Barbed wire can be easily represented by ordinary wire coiled round a pencil then opened out a little. Infantry would be held up for one move but tanks would go over it. Infantry following their tanks would also pass through unhindered. Guns could be used to blow up the wire, a hit clearing perhaps 3 in. Wire that had been destroyed would have to be marked.

Supply

No mention has been made of supply and since this is a major part of war it deserves some consideration. Supply wagons or lorries could be allocated at the rate of one to every company of infantry, or battery of artillery, or squadron of tanks. Provided the wagons remain with 6 in. of their units all supplies would be automatic but if that gap widened, or if the supply vehicle was destroyed, then the unit would only be able to fire for three more moves before running out of ammunition.

Movement

In order to save time in the first moves of a game it could be agreed between players that only the first rank of a unit need be moved. These pieces would serve to show the unit's position without having to move all the pieces. On the second moves the same method could be applied but after that the game usually begins to get too complex and it is best to abandon the system. Small trays can be made and a company of men moved as one unit, thus saving considerable time.

No allowance has been made for reserves off the field of battle. This is solved by leaving some pieces off the board at the outset of the game. Later, at a time previously agreed by the players, these reserves could be moved on to the board, advancing along the approach roads.

Another Bellona emplacement. They are light and tend to slide about, but can be weighted with platiscene.

Possible adaptations to rules

A set of morale rules could be introduced, ruled by dice and the number of pieces. If a unit is reduced to 50 per cent or less it must throw a dice to see if it will (a) stand firm—score 5 or 6. *(b)* begin to retreat—score 3 or 4. (c) turn and run— score 1 or 2.

Alternatively, discarding the dice, if a unit is reduced to two-thirds it will stop advancing; if reduced to half it will begin a fighting retreat; if reduced to one-third it will turn and run.

Both these methods entail a great deal of head counting and tend to slow up the game, especially if the armies involved are large.

An alternative to the four dice throws in mêlées is to use the method employed for firing, i.e. every 10 men would throw a dice, fractions over five counting half score, under five being disregarded. This method gives realistic results by increasing the number of casualties inflicted by the player with superior forces engaged.

Other complications that could be* introduced include different speeds for the various types of tanks, the same with other vehicles, different ranges and firepower for artillery and tanks, the difference between crossbows and long bows, the use of boiling oil, mining operations, the difference between chain mail and plate armour . . .

The list is endless and I would advise you to master the straightforward game completely before trying out the numerous complications.

Part II Wargaming Rules of Terry Wise

Over a lifetime of wargaming, Terry Wise developed his own rules to reflect his own interests. Some sets have been published, but the following sets have never reached the public domain until now.

Notes on the wargaming rules

The Napoleonic rules evolved over some 40 years (and still continue to evolve). 'Improvements', additions and revisions, have been added over these years but were always dropped because they add little to a game except complications. Archie Cass once said 'Any fool can write complicated rules!'

All the rules may be used with 15, 20 and 25mm figures; personally I usually play with 1000-2000 a side, but have used them for brigade level games, and with over 2,000 figures a side. The rules are aimed at brigade, division and corps, so are idea for solo, through to multi-player games.

Many explanations could be offered about the thinking behind these rules, but that would have taken another book. An example for artillery, in real life there was a 50% chance of hitting a target up to 600 yards (24" inches) in Napoleonic times. At 900 yards (36"), there was only a 15% chance of hitting the target. First graze of the cannon ball was usually about 400 yards (16") at 0^0 elevation, 2nd graze at about 800 yards (32") and final landing circa 900 yards. As I said, I could write a book about the reasons behind each of these rules.

I present my rules now in the hope that others may take pleasure from them as I have done.

18th Century Rules

DEFINITIONS

REGULARS: British & French Line Infantry. Rangers. Also *Coureurs des Bois*[6] but always unformed

MILITIA: Provincials, Minute Men, most Highlanders, sepoys and sowars in India

LEVIES: North American forest Indians (always unformed), Hindu and Moslem tribal levies in India

MOVEMENT

Method: measurements for movement are taken from the heads of front ranks, from centre of cannon

INFANTRY	In.	
Column	8	Highlanders in column of companies move 5 if formed, 8 if charging
Line	5	
Open order	10	
CAVALRY & Staff	12	
GALLOPERS	12	
F.A. & Gunners	8	
Pack Animals	8	
Wagons	5	

MOVE PENALTIES:
- change direction: left, right, or face about, no penalty
- change formation, rally or reform: move at slowest speed for Regulars; 1 move for all others
- broken ground: ½ speed and formed, * speed & unformed (full speed downhill)
- obstacles/woods: ½ speed and unformed (infantry only)
- buildings/fortifications: all troops move at 8 inches at all times
- limber/unlimber: 1 move, gallopers / move. 2 crew required

---

[6] A *coureur des bois* (runner of the woods) was an individual who engaged in the fur trade without permission from the French authorities.

The *coureurs des bois*, mostly of French descent, operated during the late 17th century and early 18th century in eastern North America, particularly in New France.

Later, a limited number of permits were issued to *coureurs des bois* who became known as *voyageurs*.

- Open order troops do not suffer any movement penalties

UNFORMED: caused by broken ground, obstacles, woods, pursuit, routing, caught changing formation, cavalry in mêlée, troops inside buildings

REFORMING: must be halted, not firing, not under attack (including missile attack)

ARTILLERY FIRING

	SHORT	MEDIUM	LONG
RANGE 3pdr	8	16	24
8pdr	10	20	30
SCORE TO KILL	2,3, 4,5,6	3, 4, 5, 6	5,6
CASUALTIES INF	4	2	1
CAV	2	1	1

MODIFIERS:
-1 from casualties if: 3pdr at short range in open order or in hard cover
+ 1 to casualties if enfiladed or along length of column
MOVE & FIRE: guns may NOT limber, unlimber, or change face & fire
COUNTER BATTERY: score 5 or 6 for hit.
5=gunner killed, 6=gun out of action during next move
FORTIFICATIONS: (8 pdrs only): score 6 for hit, 1 figure removed
COUNTER BATTERY: score 6 for hit (remove 1 gunner) Throw again, 5 or 6 = gun out of action during next move

SMALL ARMS FIRING

RANGE	REGULAR	MILITIA	LEVY
-4"	5	6	10
-7"	6	10	20
-10"	10	20	
-15"	20		

Method

- 1 figure removed for each group firing
- ½ casualties for all troops in open order (including gunners/engineers)
- ½ casualties in hard cover
- maximum of 2 ranks may fire, 1 rank within or from edge of woods
- once in range formed infantry may advance or retire 1 inch per move before firing without penalty
- only 8 rounds of ammunition are carried, a tally sheet is used to keep

track of ammunition used.

MOVE AND FIRE: Infantry move and fire without penalty when first engaging an opposing unit Open order troops move and fire at all times but only half the unit fires.

MELEE
Method:
- individual combats, dice scores separated by more than 1 spot to win
- charge to contact must be announced previously and must be in a straight line
- each unit charged must test morale to stand and receive charge
- 1st round, front ranks only plus 1 figure overlap at each end,
- thereafter at will open order troops may not close ranks in 1st round
- cavalry are unformed by mêlée (use status marker)
- guns being charged may evade 8 inches or stand and fire, then mêlée. Militia arty must always evade
- infantry being charged may fire (and evade if in open order) then mêlée. Regulars fire at short range, Militia at medium, Levies at long. Militia and Levies upgrade to next range up if general officer with unit

ADD 1 if Regulars
          infantry column vs inf line
          Highland charge
          attacking in flank
ADD 2 if cavalry vs infantry
          Attacking in rear
          outnumber 2:1
ADD 3 if outnumber 3:1

MINUS 1 if Levies

Note: troops attacked in flank and/or rear may not kill in 1st round, only survive.

PURSUIT

Units in mêlée which obtain a Control result for morale may choose to pursue an opposing unit which has a Recoil or worse morale result.

Pursuing units become unformed but remain under control until suffering more casualties

If a pursued unit has its back to the pursuer, 1 pursued figure is removed per move for each pursuer in contact

MORALE

Method: tested at the end of each move if suffering casualties, or when charged count % of casualties and from this:-

+ 10% if Regulars
        Highlanders charging
        Levies in woods
        Commander with unit
- 10% if unformed OR in open order Levies
- 20% if attacked in flank
- 30% if attacked in rear

Dice and consult chart:- (note uneven %'s dice, 1,2,3 go up, 4,5,6 go down)

	ROUT	WITHDRAW	RECOIL	CHECK	CONTROL
10%	-	1	2	3	456
20%	1	2	3	4	56
30%	1	23	4	5	6
40%	12	34	5	6	-
50%	rout and lost to battle				

– CHECK = can do anything except advance
– RECOIL = 1 move, face enemy, formed, no firing
– WITHDRAW = 2 moves, face enemy, unformed, no firing
– ROUT   = 2 moves, face rear, unformed, no firing (Markers used to indicate status)
An Army which has lost half its units, or its C-in-C, must withdraw from the table. This may be a fighting withdrawal

RALLYING

Units being rallied must be halted, not firing, and not under attack (including missile attack). After two moves of rout an attempt may be made to rally if general officer present:

      5,6 = rallied at 1st try
      6 = rallied at 2nd try
      +1 if Regulars -1 if Levies
Thereafter lost to battle

Rallied units coming under attack (including by missiles) must test morale every move whilst under attack

Surrounded units: as Morale result, but if result is Recoil, Withdraw or

Rout they must surrender. One guard figure is needed for every 5 captured figures

Napoleonic Wargaming Rules 1792-1815

DEFINITIONS

SCALES: 1mm = 1 yard. 1 figure = 33 actual. 1 gun = a battery (2 guns for Russia.)

OBSTACLES includes walls, hedges, ditches

TEMPLATE for artillery/infantry angle of fire should be triangles with 60° corners: if this is too generous, reduce the frontage to 50mm & so reduce the angle. L.I. & Rifles in open order do not have angle of fire restriction, except it must be to their front.

ENFILADE means firing into flank of a line, but also down the length of a column: it is *the number of figures in depth receiving fire (4 or more) that determines enfilade.*

COLUMN is 3 abreast for infantry, 2 abreast for cavalry.

LINE is 2 or 3 ranks deep for infantry, cavalry deploy by squadron frontage in single line.

OPEN ORDER may only be used by L.I., Rifles & Light Cavalry (not Lancers) & should be spaced so that another figure could be inserted between each pair.

GUNNERS/ENGINEERS count as close order when limbered up, open order when deployed round gun or engineering work.

MARKERS of appropriate size may be used for all units not visible to the enemy C-in-C figure. If visible to another general figure, that information must be sent to the C-in-C before the marker is revealed. 1 dummy marker may be used for every 5 real ones.

EQUIPMENT: rules, 2 or 3 D6, average dice, D10, 3" burst circle for howitzers.

GENERALS must touch centre base of a unit to count as with it. If a general in mêlée has 2:1 & loses, the other figure is removed. Generals melee as Heavy Cavalry.

ARTILLERY firing canister at infantry with skirmisher screen takes casualties 2:1
      -behind hard cover counts as in fortifications (except against howitzers)

ATTACKED IN FLANK OR REAR includes receiving artillery fire thus.

CHARGES charge speed only used if ends in melee. Col vs Line refers to infantry only.

MORALE IN CHARGES: count entire unit even if not all components are engaged at first.

LANCERS move as Light Cavalry but melee as Medium.

CAVALRY, in line may engage as individual squadrons: varying squadron deployment is not a change of formation.
If a unit type is not available, nothing appears that move: alternatively, the player tries again.

BRIGADE DEPLOYMENT: as above but Infantry Brigade 80 max: Cavalry Brigade 50 max; Artillery 2 guns max. Variations in troop type are at player's choice. Generals in proportion - 1 per brigade.

SEVEN YEARS WAR VARIANT TO RULES
delete rifles;
3-6pdrs move as FA;
all other guns as 12rdrs.

Movement

Method: all measurements taken from/to men's heads, teams' noses, gun trunnions.

Unit Type		Charge	Open Order
Infantry	Line 5" Column 8"	8"	8"
Light Cavalry	14"	18"	14"
Lancers	14"	18"	-
Medium Cavalry	12"	16"	-
Heavy cavalry	10"	14"	-
Horse Artillery	12"	-	-
Field Artillery	8"	-	-
Staff	18 at all times		

ARTILLERY MANOEUVRES: min 2 crew at all times		
	Limber/ unlimber	Prolonge[7]
Horse artillery	½ move	2½ & fire
Field artillery	½ move	3 pdr only -2½ & fire
12 pdr	1 move	-

Artillery is considered unloaded if attacked while moving

Gunners away from guns move 8" at all times

---

[7] a specially fitted rope used as part of the towing equipment of a gun carriage

MOVE & FIRE:

Horse ½ move, unlimber & fire
Field artillery 12pdrs may not fire after moving or changing front

Bonuses
    -roads: add 2" on roads if infantry or guns
    – Changing position: all troops may move 1" to side or rear without penalty

PENALTIES

change direction	about face or wheel once per move without penalty
change formation	1 move on spot for Guards/Line, 2 moves for Militia
broken ground/hills	½ speed
obstacles/woods	½ speed, infantry & open order troops
streams/fords	½ speed
fortifications:	½ speed to enter/leave, 8" within them at all times
Infantry squares:	2" in any direction, or 1" and fire

ARTILLERY FIRING

Method: direct line of sight only & within angle of template.

Restrictions
- no firing within 2" of own troops.
- no overhead firing except howitzers (6" clear of own troops, hills, woods)
- Howitzers can use observation post chain to observe targets, max 6" spacing.
- if crew strength ½ or less, fire every other move

Ball	Range
3 pdr	Upto 20"
6 pdr	Upto 25"
8-9 pdr	Upto 30"
12 pdr	Upto 35"

SCORE TO HIT
automatic if in square
2-6 if in line
3-6 if column, broken ground, woods
4, 5, 6 if open order or hard cover

Effect 1 killed + 1 if target in column/ enfilade/ square
Canister: automatic hit

	Range	Effect		
		Cav	Inf	Open order/ in woods/ hard cover
All guns	3"	1	2	1
	9"	2	3	1
12 pdr	12"	1	2	1

Shell (howitzers only)   Range 12" min 35" max
estimate range & name precise point of aim
–measure only to estimated range & dice for linear error
  1 = misfire
  2 = left
  3,4,5 = hit
  6 = right
  error is 2" up to 24" 3" up to 35"
–centre 3" burst circle over hit point & remove casualties:-

close order	3 infantry	2 cavalry	2 gunners
open order	2 infantry	1 cavalry	1 gunner
use open order rate if in woods			

Hits on teams or limbers = destroyed

Counter Battery fire *check range and dice for hit*

Gun	Short	Medium	Long	Modifiers
3 pdr	5	15	20	+ 1 to score if target
6 pdr	10	20	25	limbered up
8-9 pdr	15	25	30	+ if 12 pdr to score
12 pdr	20	30	35	firing
Score to hit	3-6	4,5,6	6	

Effect

Vs gun *dice again*   1,2,3,4 = 1 crew killed

  5 = gun out of action for 1 move

  6 = gun out of action for 2 moves

Vs limber *dice again*   1,2 = team killed

  3,4 = immobilized

  5,6 = explodes

Vs gun in fortifications *3 pdrs have no effect*

  Dice again   3, 4, 5 = 1 crew killed

  6 = gun out of action:

Vs doors/ gates/ fortifications hit = 25mm width destroyed (*3 pdrs have no effect*)

Infantry Firing

Method check for the weapon range used, remove casualties as per the table below. Odd figure casualties are ignored.

Line infantry may take ½ move and fire (or visa versa).

Light infantry must in open order to use the light infantry fire table. The may make ½ move and fire.

Rifle armed infantry must be in at least 2 ranks. Only ½ may fire each turn (due to the speed of reloading). They may make ½ move and fire.

Rifles/ Light infantry in close order move and fire as line infantry

Formed troops in line are in 3 ranks to fire, except for the British/ Portuguese who fire in 2 ranks

Troops in column may fire 2 ranks (at the head of the column) at 4" or above when charging. Charging columns may take full charge move and fire at 4" *only* if they have not fired on the previous move.

Restrictions angle of fire must be at target within 45^0 of front of the unit and the target may not be within 2" of own troops.

No firing overhead of other troops

May fire 3" within woods, but only 1" from/ into edge of woods (*woods are often thicker at their edge*)

Each group of men firing kills 1, plus or minus the modifiers. E.g. 8 guard infantry firing at 3" kill 2 figures.

Muskets: number firing			
Range	Guard	Infantry	Militia
0-3"	4	5	6
Upto 4"	5	6	7
Upto 6"	6	8	10
Upto 8"	8	10	-

Light Infantry Muskets		Rifles	
Range	Number firing	Range	Number firing
0-4"	5	0-5"	2
Upto 7"	6	Upto 10"	3
Upto 10"	7	Upto 15"	4

CHARGES

Method
-must be announced before moves start & must be in a straight line
-attacks veering from a straight line may not use charge speed or charge bonus
 -those charging must test morale if receiving fire during charge (not at 3" or less)
-those charged must test morale if chargers not stopped by the firing
-close order infantry being charged may fire then melee: each battalion throws an average dice, plus or minus for range:-

Add 1 if	Guard unit General with unit	Minus 1 if	moved before firing Militia Received artillery fire On previous move

Score =	Fire at
5	Upto 3"
4	Upto 4"
3	Upto 5"
2	Upto 6"

FORMED TROOPS vs open order: if open order troops can find cover (walls, trees, rocks, limbers etc) they may stand, fire, & even melee, otherwise they run to their nearest support unit. If such a unit is not reached in time they may be cut down -1 figure killed for each figure in pursuit & in contact each move.

CHARGING GUNS:

Vs formed cavalry	4,5,6 = fire canister	1,2,3 = run to nearest support
Vs formed infantry	4,5,6 = fire canister	1,2,3 = run to nearest support
Vs Open order cavalry	3,4,5,6 = fire canister	1,2 = run to nearest support
Open order infantry	Players choice	

If gunners fire & melee ensues - gunners may not kill in 1st round of melee, only survive. If gunners run, chargers may pursue them beyond the guns. Pursuit rules then apply. Cavalry would normally kill limber teams: takes 1 move of melee at 1 man per horse.

MELEE

Method:-individual combats, dice scores separated by more than 1 spot to win e.g. if one figure rolled a 4 and the other a 2, the figure rolling 4 would kill the other figure.

-1st round of combat front ranks only, +1 figure overlap each end, 2nd and subsequent rounds, all figures may join in.

-column charging line may double its frontage each move after 1st round

-gunners count as Line Infantry, staff as Heavy Cavalry

Add 1	Add 2	Add 3
Charging	H. Cav vs L. Cav	If M.Cav v infantry
Column vs line (1st move)	L.Cav vs infantry	Outnumbered 3:1
Guard	Outnumbers 2:1	**Add 4**
H.Cav vs M.Cav	Attacking enemy in rear	H.Cav v infantry
M.Cav vs L.Cav		**Minus 1**
Lancers		Militia
Attacking in flank		Defender behind hard cover

There is no charge bonus against troops behind hardcover

Troops attacked in flank &/or rear may not kill in 1st round, only survive

If defender behind cover is killed, attacker crosses cover to engage on equal terms next round.

Pursuit

LOSER OF MELEE tests morale If fails, winner tests for pursuit If not pursuing, winner tests morale	Dice 1,2=must pursue 3,4=no pursuit 5,6= player's choice	**ADD 1** if Guard General with unit **MINUS** 1 if militia

Do not check for pursuit for Recoil: melee may be continued or broken off, players' choice.

Unengaged squadrons of cavalry regiments do not have to test for pursuit.

Cavalry do not have to pursue over obstacles (including guns/limbers), through woods, or into a new enemy unit - player's choice

If a pursued unit has its back to the pursuer, 1 figure is killed for every move the pursuer is in contact

Pursuit is tested every move in contact & is always at charge speed

Lost to Battle troops, are pursued as normal but may be removed from the table if not pursued.

Pursuit off edge of table: pursuer does not follow off the table but must withdraw to nearest friendly forces at charge speed

MORALE

Method: tested at the end of each move if suffering casualties, charged, or charging

–count % of casualties & to this ADD or MINUS then consult chart:-

%	ROUT	RETREAT	W'DRAW	RECOIL	CHECK	SLOWED	CONTROL
10%	-	-	-	-	1	2	3-6
15%	-	-	-	-	1	2,3	4,5,6
20%	-	-	1	2	3	4	5,6
25%	-	1	2	3	4	5	6
30%	1	2	3	4	5	6	-
35%	1,2	3,4	5,6	-	-	-	-
40%	1,2,3	4,5	6	-	-	-	-
45%	1-4	5,6	-	-	-	-	-
50%	Lost to battle						

Add 10%	if Guard or Rifles
	General with unit
Add 20%	If C-in-c with unit
	In hard cover
Minus 10%	if Militia
Minus 20%.	if attacked in flank
Minus 30%	if attacked in rear

SLOWED = can do anything, but always at ½ speed
CHECK = can do anything except advance or attack
RECOIL = ½ move back, slowest speed, face enemy, may fire
WITHDRAW = 1 move back, slowest speed, face enemy, no firing
RETREAT = 1 move back column speed, face rear, no firing
Rout = 1½ moves back at charge speed, face rear, no firing or fighting. May only rally/reform after 1½ moves & must be by a general. May only survive in melée

LOST TO BATTLE = if at ½ strength or over at end of Rout moves may be rallied & reformed by a general.

RALLY/REFORM: score 4,5,6 Guard, 5,6 Line, 6 Militia. Take next move to reform. Rallied units coming under attack (including by artillery) must test morale every move whilst under attack & therefore need a general with them.

ROUT/RETREAT/WITHDRAW/RECOIL must be taken directly to rear for 1st move, disrupting any friendly units in their path. Thereafter they may go round flanks of friendly units, breaking up at will

SURROUNDED UNITS cannot Recoil/Withdraw/Retreat & must surrender: 1 guard figure per 5 captured figures or part thereof

An Army which has lost its C-in-C, or half its units, must withdraw from the table. This may take the form of a fighting withdrawal.

Unit Strength	-10%	-15%	-20%	-25%	-30%	-35%	-40%	-45%	-50%
10	9	-	8	-	7	-	6	-	5
15	14	13	12	-	11	10	9	8	7
16	14	14	13	12	11	10	10	9	8
18	16	15	14	13	13	12	11	10	9
20	18	17	16	15	14	13	12	11	10
25	23-22	21	20	19	18-17	16	15	14	13-12
30	27	26-25	24	23-22	21	20-19	18	17-16	15
32*	29-28	27	26-25	24	23-22	21-20	19	18-17	16
40*	36	34	32	30	28	26	24	22	20

*Regiments of 2 battalions may take morale at regimental strength if battalions are within 2" of each other, or they may take morale on individual battalions. This decision cannot be reversed later.

N.B. Where strengths appear as double numbers, or there is a gap in the numbering, dice to go up (4,5,6) or down (1,2,3)

Ney commanding the rear guard in the French retreat from Moscow

Colonial Rules 1874 – 1914

THESE RULES were written specifically for the wars in India and Africa listed below, but can be used for many other colonial wars of the period.

1877-78 9th Kaffir War
1880-81 1st Boer War
1882-85 Egypt and the Sudan
1884- German South West Africa
1882-85 Egypt and the Sudan
1884- German South West Africa
1885-90 German East Africa
1896 Matabele Uprising
1896-97 Malakand Campaign
1896-98 Egypt and the Sudan
1897-98 Tirah Campaign
1899-1902 2nd Boer War

DEFINITIONS

REGULARS: British and German troops, British Colonial and Indian troops, Sudanese and Askaris, Mahdist cavalry/camelry and Boers.

NATIVES: Zulus, Egyptian and Mahdist infantry including Bashi Bazouks, Natal Native Contingents, and other native levies accompanying regular forces

MOUNTAIN GUNS: move as pack animals. They did not come into service until 1880.

HEAVY ARTILLERY: anything bigger than F.A. and including 4.7" (45pdr), and Creusot 155mm (96pdr) guns.

CO close order

OO open order = unformed, loose and irregular spacing, usual formation for massed native infantry and cavalry

EO extended order = one base space or more between figures.

CHARGES: charge speed may only be used if it takes a unit into mêlée. Units do not have to be formed to charge.

GUNNERS/ENGINEERS: formed in CO but OO when deployed for

working.

ENFILADE: firing into the flank of a line, but also down the length of a column: it is the number of figures in depth receiving fire (4 or more) that determines enfilade.

GENERALS must touch centre base of a unit to count as with it. If a general in mêlée has 2:1 and loses, the other figure is removed.
    Generals mêlée as Heavy Cavalry.

FLAG BEARERS: if these are killed it is assumed another picks up the flag.

MORALE IN CHARGES: count all components of a unit in a charge, even if part is not engaged initially.

MAHDIST GUNS: used only in fortifications, hard cover, not on battlefields. Local shells were poor with a range of only 500 yards/20".

AMMO: small arms unlimited: MG limited to 8 game moves (carried 14-16 belts=4000 rounds, average RPM was 500) = 8 moves. Artillery limited to 16 rounds, player's choice of shell or case, (11 shell to 5 case is the norm).

SCOUTING: natives always out-scouted Regulars. Therefore Regulars should be placed on the table, but Natives use markers which are only placed on table as the figures become visible or are revealed by scouting.

MARKERS of appropriate size may be used for all units not visible to the opposing C-in-C figure. If visible to another general figure, that information must be conveyed to the C-in-C by a figure. In the case of Natives, small markers may be used under rocks, trees or hexes etc., or marked on a map of the layout. One dummy marker may be used for every five real ones.

EQUIPMENT: ruler, D6 dice, D10 dice, 2" 3" 5" 7" burst circles.

TEMPLATES for artillery/infantry angle of fire should be triangles with 60° corners: if this is too generous, reduce the front edge to 50mm and so reduce the angles. Open order troops do not have an angle of fire restriction, except it must be to their front.

OBSTACLES include walls, hedges and ditches.

MOVEMENT

Method: all measurements taken from/to men's heads, noses of teams, trunnions of guns

Troop type	CO	OO	EO	Charge	Square
Regular Infantry	5"	7"	9"	8"	2"
Regular Cavalry	8	10	12	14	-
Native Infantry	8	10	12	12	-
Native Cavalry	10	12	14	16	-
Camelry	12	14	16	18	-
Field Artillery and Machine Guns	8	At all times			
Pack Animals	8				
Wagons	5				
Heavy artillery	5				
Staff	14				

Add 2" on roads for all infantry, cavalry and camelry

Artillery Moves: need minimum of 2 crew at all times			
Gun	Unlimber	Limber	Prolonge*
Field Artillery/ MG	½ move	½ move	2½" & fire
Mountain	1 move	1 move	2½" & fire
Heavy	1 move	2 moves	-
Gunners away from guns move 8" at all times			

*Unloaded if attacked while moving

MOVEMENT PENALTIES

-change direction: about face or wheel once per move without penalty

-change formation/reform: ½ move on centre for British, 1 move for all others

-mount/dismount/& deploy: ½ move.
    Horseholders required 1:4 except Boers

–broken ground/ obstacles/ woods:
    Infantry/Wagons 2"
    Artillery/Pack 3"
    Cavalry/Camelry 4"
(except Mahdist and Zulu infantry who do not suffer penalties unless in CO, when as others)

- streams/fords: ½ speed and unformed
- fortifications/buildings: ½ move to enter/leave 8 inches within them, unformed

ARTILLERY FIRING

Method: direct line of sight only and within angle of template

Restrictions: no firing within 2 inches of own troops
no overhead firing at under 12 inches: at greater ranges only from higher ground

SHELL: no range limit.

Burst circle:
    Mountain 2 inces
    Field Artillery 3 inches
    Heavy 5 inches

- estimate range and name precise point of aim
- measure only to estimated range and dice for linear deviation
    1 = left 3 inches
    6 = right 3 inches
    2,3,4,5 = hit
– place centre of burst circle over hit point and remove casualties

Close order	5 infantry	3 cavalry	2 gunners
Open order / in woods	3	2	1
extended	1	1	-

Counter Battery fire: use shell, case and machine gun effects on crews and teams.

Machine Guns: check range, remove casualties as per table below

Ranges	CO		OO/ in woods		EO/ target in hard cover/ buildings	
	Inf	Cav	Inf	Cav	Inf	Cav
20	5	3	4	2	3	1
40	4	2	3	1	2	1
60	3	2	2	1	1	1
90	2	1	1	1	1	1

Gatling Gun jams: dice D10 every move of firing
    1 = jams for 2 moves (i.e. resume firing on third move)
    Jams cannot be cleared if crew are in mêlée

Case shot

Ranges	CO		OO/ in woods		EO/ target in hard cover/ buildings	
	Inf	Cav	Inf	Cav	Inf	Cav
3"	3	2	4	1	1	1
6"	5	3	3	2	1	1
9"	5	3	3	2	1	1
12"	2	1	2	1	1	1

INFANTRY FIRING

Method: check range for weapon used, remove casualties as effects table, odd figure discounted

– units may take 1/2 move and fire or vice versa, or may stand and fire once per move - maximum of 2 ranks may fire in all formations

– British may use volley fire up to 32 inches (40 inches post 1891) but only if entire unit is in close order, formed, and not moving

Restrictions:

– angle of fire within template and not within 2 inches of own troops
– no overhead firing at short range: at other ranges only from higher ground
– may fire up to 3 inches within woods, up to 1 inch from or into the edge of woods
– ambush: those surprised (including from woods and buildings) may only return fire after removing casualties inflicted and testing morale

Troop Type	Range (inches)			
	Short	Medium	Long	Maximum
Indian/ Egyptian pre-1891	12	24	36	48
British pre-1891	16	32	40	60
Indian/ Egyptian post 1891/ Cavalry Carbines	16	32	26	40
Zulu/ Mahdist spearmen	Throw as mêlée			
British post 1891	20	40	60	90
Boers/ Germans	24	48	64	90

CHARGES

Method: must be announced at start of move and must be in straight line.
- those charging must test morale if receiving fire during charge (not 6 inches or under)
- those charged must test morale if chargers not stopped by firing
- infantry being charged may fire then mêlée

FORMED TROOPS vs extended order: if EO troops can find cover (walls, rocks, trees, limbers etc) they may stand, fire and even mêlée, otherwise they run to nearest support unit. If such a unit is not reached in time they are cut down - 1 figure killed for each figure in pursuit and in contact each move.

CHARGING GUNS

Gunners dice

Charged by	Fire case	run to support
Formed cavalry	5, 6	1, 2, 3, 4
Formed infantry	4, 5, 6	1, 2, 3
Open order cavalry	3, 4, 5, 6	1, 2
Open order infantry	player's choice	

+ 1 to score if British/ German
− 1 if natives

Mêlée or pursuit ensues: gunners who have fired may not kill in 1st round, only survive. Cavalry would normally kill limber teams - takes 1 move of mêlée at 1 man per horse

Mêlée

Method:- individual combats, dice scores separated by more than 1 spot to win
-1st round front ranks only, troops not in formation may swarm round flanks to the limit of their move
-gunners count as infantry, staff as cavalry

ADD 1	If charging+	ADD 2	if Zulu/Mahdist vs Native Inf
	Attack in flank*		Cav vs Inf in OO or EO
	British vs Boers		attacking in rear
	Cav vs Inf in CO (1st only)		outnumber 2:1
	Regular cav vs other cavalry	ADD 3	if outnumber 3:1
	Lance or spear armed (not assegai)		

*troops attacked in flank and/or rear may not kill in 1st round but may only survive
+ not vs troops behind hard cover

Capturing horses: any figure in contact unopposed may capture 1 horse per move up to a maximum of 4

Stampeding horses: each hit on unattended horse stampedes 4 other horses nearby,

Pursuit

Loser of mêlée: tests morale.
    If fails, winner tests for pursuit
    If not pursuing, winner tests morale
Dice for pursuit as per the table.

Troop type	Pursue	No pursuit	Player's choice
British	1	2	3, 4, 5, 6
Native	1-4	5	6
Other	1, 2	3, 4	5, 6

ADD 1 to score if general with unit

Cavalry do not have to pursue over obstacles, through woods, or into a new enemy - player's choice. If not pursuing, charge speed back to friendly units.

If a pursued unit has its back to a pursuer, 1 figure is removed every move for each pursuer in contact.

MORALE

Method: tested at the end of each move if suffering casualties, or if charging or being charged. Count % of casualties suffered and to or from this ADD or MINUS, then dice and consult the chart for results.

ADD 10%	British/German	MINUS 10%	if EO and over 8" from supports
	charging		natives suffering arty losses
	in square		receiving volley fire
	general with unit		loss of general
	natives attacking Regulars who are withdrawing		Boer line of retreat threatened
ADD 20%	in hard cover/buildings	MINUS 20%	if attacked in flank ambushed
	natives in mêlée with Regulars	MINUS 30%	if attacked in rear

%	Rout	Retreat	W'draw	Recoil	Check	Slowed	Control
10%	-	-	-	-	1	2	3-6
15%	-	-	-	-	1	2, 3	4-6
20%	-	-	1	2	3	4	5, 6
25%	-	1	2	3	4	5	6
30%	1	2	3	4	5	6	-
35%	1, 2	3, 4	5, 6	-	-	-	-
40%	1-3	4, 5	6	-	-	-	-
45%	1-4	5, 6	-	-	-	-	-
50%	Lost to battle						

SLOWED = can do anything but always at ½ speed

CHECK = can do anything except advance or attack

RECOIL move back, slowest speed, face enemy, may fire

W'DRAW = 1 move back, slowest speed, face enemy, no firing

RETREAT= 1 move back, fastest speed, face rear, no firing

ROUT = 1½ moves back, fastest speed, face rear, no fighting or firing.

May only rally/reform after 1½ moves and must be rallied by a general. May only survive in mêlée (fights to survive but may not kill

LOST TO BATTLE = if at ½ strength or over at end of Rout moves may be rallied and reformed by a general:-

RALLY/REFORM: score 4, 5, 6 British/German Regulars, 6 Natives, 5, 6 all others. Take next move to reform. Rallied units coming under attack (including by artillery) must test morale every move while under attack and therefore will always need a general with them

Rout/Retreat/Withdraw/Recoil must be taken directly to rear for 1st move, disrupting any formed friendly units in their path. Thereafter may go round flanks of such units, breaking up at will.

Troops in buildings obtaining Withdraw/Retreat result may fight on, but if Rout they must surrender.

Surrounded units obtaining Recoil/Withdraw/Retreat/Rout result must surrender. 1 guard figure is required for every 5 captured figures or part thereof.

An.army which has lost half its units or its C-in-C must withdraw from the table. This may take the form of a fighting withdrawal.